CLANS
COOK BOOK

GLAYVA
CLANS
COOK BOOK

Favourite Family Recipes of Scotland's Clan Chiefs

Compiled by Wendy Jones

Foreword by The Earl of Elgin and Kincardine

Macdonald Publishers • Edinburgh

Published by
Macdonald Publishers
Edgefield Road, Loanhead
Midlothian, EH20 9SY

ISBN   0 904265 47 1

Printed in Scotland by
Macdonald Printers (Edinburgh) Ltd
Edgefield Road, Loanhead
Midlothian, EH20 9SY

Designed and edited by Jenny Carter

Photographs by Nick Price

Acknowledgements

My thanks to Scotland's Clan Chiefs and Heads of Families who have contributed the recipes in this book (as well as their wives, families, relatives and cooks who normally prepare the recipes).

I am grateful to James S. Adam of the Scottish International Gathering Trust Ltd., whose enthusiasm for my idea of the *Clans Cook Book* encouraged me to produce it.

Thanks also to The Standing Council of Scottish Chiefs, who have guided me through the jungle of Clan titles; The National Trust for Scotland, The Duke of Atholl, The Earl of Elgin and Major Borthwick of Borthwick who allowed us to invade their estates and homes for location photography; Jenners of Princes Street, Edinburgh (and Jane Gibbons), for providing so much of the china, glass, kitchen ware and accessories used in photography; Heron-Rossleigh of Edinburgh (and Bill Bryson) for the Range Rover used in photography; Rhona Howat for typing the manuscript.

Queen Margaret College, Edinburgh

The majority of the recipes in this book have been tried, tested and tasted by the post-graduate Home Economics students at Edinburgh's Queen Margaret College.

The students, Carole Hoskins and Eileen Hunter, led by their course tutor Miss Alison Reid, have worked on the *Clans Cook Book* as a practical exercise, culminating in the preparation of the food for photography as well as assisting the photographer in studio and location shots.

I am most grateful to the students for their assistance, and for their "cook's comments."

Contents

Foreword	7	MacDougall	69
		Mackay	72
Introduction	9	Mackenzie	74
		MacKinnon	76
Oven temperatures and		Mackintosh	78
measurement chart	10	MacLean	79
		MacLennan	83
Agnew	13	MacLeod	84
Arbuthnott	15	Macmillan	86
Barclay	16	Macnaghten	88
Borthwick	18	Macneil	90
Boyle	20	Macpherson	92
Brodie	23	MacThomas	94
Bruce	24	Malcolm	98
Buchan	26	Matheson	99
Cameron	28	Menzies	103
Carnegie	30	Moncreiffe	104
Chisholm	32	Morrison	106
Cochrane	36	Murray	108
Cranston	38	Ogilvy	110
Cumming	40	Ramsay	112
Drummond	42	Rattray	113
Elliot	44	Robertson	114
Erskine	45	Rollo	116
Farquharson	46	Rose	118
Forbes	48	Scott	120
Fraser	51	Shaw	122
Grant	54	Stirling	125
Gunn	55	Sutherland	126
Haig	56	Urquhart	128
Hamilton	57	Wallace	133
Hay	58		
Keith	59	Recipes from Glayva	135
Leslie	60		
MacBain	62	Glayva drinks	140
Macdonald	66		
Macdonald of Clanranald	68	Index	141

Foreword

The Earl of Elgin and Kincardine, D.L., J.P.

"Contented wi' little and canty wi' mair."

This well-used aphorism sums up much of the content of this agreeable book. Another time-honoured feature is the frequent recurrence of fish recipes. This, in itself, is a fascinating historical side-line because, in the records of Parliament, from the time of King Robert I, a similar pattern can be seen. The "top people" of the 14th century ate their way through thousands of herring, eels and salmon; even a dolphin appeared on the occasion of a Parliament held at Clackmannan, the home of the Bruces. But cattle, bacon, pork and mutton, although available in numbers, were (in weight), about half. Then, when they had eaten all that was available, they adjourned—for the simple fact was that there was no more to be had! This system of larder-to-plate still appears in these present-day suggestions, although can and deep-freeze have taken the place of salt and ice-house.

There is also a frugal element of reconstitution in some of these recipes; reminiscent of the Minister of the Kirk who failed to bless the dinner which his wife had set before him—when she remonstrated at his failure, he replied that it had all been blessed before.

The truth is that in the past decade we, in Scotland, have become omnivorous, and we accept much that would have been rejected—as Robert Burns remarked—as trash. Yet, in all that we think we have learned from other places and other lands, we still love

---

Opposite: The cupboard on which I am carving the lamb is an old Dutch oak chest, lined (in about 1850) with sheet tin and heated with a hot brick. In 1909-10 the brick was replaced by an electric warmer made by Lieutenant The Hon. John Bruce, RN, then on board *HMS Lion.* The capacity is at least enough for fourteen people and no food is ever spoiled in it, even if kept for 3-4 hours.

The mantlepiece was constructed out of the surviving pieces of the nuptial bed brought to Scotland by Princess Anne of Denmark, bride of James VI. The 9th Earl, who carried out this work in the latter part of the 19th century, always felt it amusing that Charles I should have been born on his dining-room mantlepiece.

our "hamely fare", whether we live in a stately seat or in a more modest dwelling.

The food of which this book speaks in such eloquent terms is only the lovely catalyst for the personal friendships and wide-ranging common interests which spring from a lunch or dinner given to our visitors, whether kinsmen or strangers, when we have the honour and pleasure of their company in our homes. So, friendly readers, serve away. Who knows? One day you, too, may become empurpled by the majesty of your cooking.

Introduction

This is a family cookery book, but one with a difference. The families are the clans and families from the Highlands and Lowlands of Scotland, the subject of historic, dramatic and romantic writings for centuries.

The *Clans Cook Book* adds another dimension to the documentation of these families. Through these pages we survey their eating habits in days gone by, and are invited to share the favourite recipes of the present Chiefs or heads of the families, giving us a glimpse of their current lifestyle. The collection which has emerged is unique in that it covers a span of some 400 years, and in so doing paints a new picture of Scots in many parts of the world.

The modern recipes will reveal the cosmopolitan tastes of these Scottish families as well as the emphasis they put on local produce. "Local produce" tends to be venison from the hills, salmon from the rivers, trout from the lochs, grouse from the moors and shell-fish from the sea. Although a number of recipes deal with this produce in its finest form, there are also those which use the equivalent of the "scrag end." The difference between these "economy" recipes in the *Clans Cook Book* and in other cookery books is that the "ends" are of venison or salmon!

I am reminded of the tale of two farm workers whom the Laird wanted to reward for their loyal service over many years. He sent them off to London for a few days to attend the famous Smithfield Fatstock Show, booking them into one of London's fine hotels.

When they returned to the Highland estate a few days later, they couldn't stop talking about this strange place called London and spoke in amazement of the prices being charged for transport, food and clothing.

"But we didnae try to tak' advantage of your generosity, sir," they said to the Laird. "We just kept to our usual plain fare in the restaurant—the salmon, the venison and the grouse."

The family favourites do include plain fare, such as Bread and Butter Pudding, Granny's Scotch Broth and Steak and Kidney Pudding, but spice has been added in the form of the anecdotes which accompany a number of the contributions.

I hope you will find that dinner party conversation can be enlivened by the retelling of some of these tales.

Wendy Jones

9

Oven Temperatures

°F	°C	Gas Mark	Temperature
250	130	½	very cool
275	140	1	very cool
300	150	2	cool
325	160	3	warm
	170		
350	180	4	moderate
375	190	5	fairly hot
400	200	6	fairly hot
425	210	7	hot
	220		
450	230	8	very hot
475	240	9	very hot

Spoon Measurements

1 teaspoon = 5 mls
4 teaspoons = approximately 1 tablespoon
1 tablespoon = approximately 20 mls
1 rounded spoon = 2 level spoons

Food	Level spoons to 1 oz (25 g) (approximate equivalents)
Flour, cornflour and other starch powders	2 tablespoons
Fresh breadcrumbs and cake crumbs	4 tablespoons
Rolled oats	3 tablespoons
Rice	2 tablespoons
Sugar	2 tablespoons
Sultanas, seedless raisins, currants	2 tablespoons
Butter	2 tablespoons
Gelatine	3 tablespoons
Syrup, treacle, honey	1 tablespoon

Handy Cup Measures

British

1 breakfast cup = approximately 10 fl oz (275-280 mls)
1 average teacup = approximately 7 fl oz (200 mls)

Food	*Weight of Average teacup in oz (g)*
Flour, cornflour, and other starch powders	4 oz (100 g)
Fresh breadcrumbs and cake crumbs	3 oz (75 g)
Oats, rolled	4 oz (100 g)
Rice	4 oz (100 g)
Sugar	6 oz (150 g)
Sultanas, seedless raisins, currants	5 oz (125 g)
Syrup, treacle, honey	14 oz (400 g)

American

American cup = approximately 8 fl oz (230 mls)
1 American cup of flour = 6 oz (150 g)
1 American cup of sugar = 8 oz (200 g)

The above measurements should be applied to the recipes under the MacBain, MacNeil and Urquhart clans.

1 gill = ¼ pint
1 quart = 2 pints
1 pint = 20 fl oz (560 mls)
½ pint = 10 fl oz (280-300 mls)
¼ pint = 5 fl oz (150 mls)

1 oz = approximately 25 g
4 oz = approximately 100 g
1 lb = approximately 500 g
2 lbs = approximately 1000 g

Agnew

From Sir Crispin Agnew of Lochnaw, Edinburgh

I first made Whisky Sour in Kathmandu for a party we were giving after the Army Expedition to Nuptse in 1975. It was so effective that guests who were expected to leave at 8.00 p.m. were still with us at 4.00 a.m. In the hot weather I had bought ice from the local ice factory, which was sold in 100 cwt. blocks. I asked them to crush it for me, which they happily agreed to do—I heard it being crushed and went out to find two bare-footed men on the mud pavement crushing the ice with rocks and then shovelling it into our containers. The doctor said the whisky would kill 99% of all known germs.

From my early days on a farm in Africa, the free-range scraggy African chick has been a staple part of my diet. The Orange Casserole gives a new dimension to battery chickens and was about the only dish that, as a bachelor, I was able to cook. At a dinner party I gave, one young lady was so horrified at the result that she has now become my wife and does all the cooking!

Whisky Sour

whisky, fresh lemon juice, soda water,
   in equal quantities
white of egg (3 whites per bottle
   of whisky)
syrup (made up from white sugar and
   water)

Mix together the whisky and lemon juice, fold in the white of egg and syrup. Stir vigorously. Just before serving add the soda water. If lemon juice is not available, use bitter lemon in lieu of juice and soda water.

13

Chicken and Orange Casserole

1 chicken, jointed
1 oz seasoned flour
2 tablespoons corn oil
1 medium onion
juice from one large orange

strips/rind cut from the skin of 1 orange
4 oz button mushrooms
1 chicken stock cube
chopped parsley

Coat the chicken in flour. Heat the oil and sauté the chicken until golden brown, remove and put in a casserole. Chop the onion, sauté, and add the remaining flour. Make up the orange juice to 1 pint with water and add to the pan with the stock cube. Bring to the boil and stir well. Add the button mushrooms and half the orange rind strips. Pour the sauce over the chicken and cook in the oven (350°F, 180°C, Gas 4) for one hour, or until tender. Garnish with the remainder of rind, and parsley.

Seal Hoosh

Take one seal, skin and strip the blubber. Make a blubber stove and slowly smoke the seal meat in a tin. Add sea water to liquefy, wait three weeks until you are very, very hungry and reheat for eating.

Editor: *While he was a major with the Royal Highland Fusiliers, Sir Crispin Agnew led the Army Mountaineering Association's expeditions to Greenland, Patagonia and to the 23,399 ft. peak Mount Api in Nepal. Sir Crispin was also on the successful Army expedition which conquered Mount Everest, not as camp cook as you might have guessed, but as official cameraman!*

Arbuthnott

From The Viscount of Arbuthnott, Laurencekirk

___

This favourite family broth was, traditionally, made entirely from ingredients available locally. The origin of the name goes back 500 years. An Arbuthnott hunting party murdered an unpopular Sheriff of the Mearns and were alleged to have put him in a huge cauldron, boiled him up and finally supped the brew!

Any vegetables in season were used, herbs were either picked in the garden or, in earlier times, gathered wild by the river bank. Any kind of meat can be used for stock—only Sheriffs need boiling for two hours!—venison, hare or an old game bird will do.

Sheriff Soup

2 lbs vegetables—for example:	2 oz butter
2 onions	2 pints stock
2 carrots	bouquet garni
1 leek	salt and pepper
1 potato	6 oz cream or creamy milk
	parsley

Chop the vegetables finely. Melt the butter in a large heavy saucepan on a low heat. Add the vegetables to the pan and toss gently until slightly soft (about 10 minutes). Add stock, bouquet garni, salt and freshly ground pepper. Simmer until the vegetables are tender (about 30-40 minutes). Remove the bouquet garni, cool slightly and sieve (or blend in a liquidiser). Return to the pan, add cream and reheat without boiling. Serve, sprinkled with fresh, chopped parsley.

___

Editor: *This must be my favourite soup recipe in the book, if only for the story I can tell at the dinner table.*

___

Barclay

From Peter C. Barclay of Towie Barclay and of that Ilk, London

---

I'm no cook although I enjoy good food, so two of the following recipes have come from my cousin, Miss E. Grant of Kemnay in Aberdeenshire. Potted shrimps is one of my favourite hors d'oeuvres and comes from the Caledonian Hotel in Edinburgh.

Cold Orange Soufflé

4 tablespoons sliced, diced sponge cake
4 tablespoons Grand Marnier
4 eggs, separated
4 oz sugar
½ pint double cream

grated rind of one orange
2 tablespoons orange juice
scant ½ oz gelatine
powdered chocolate

Soak the diced sponge cake in 2 tablespoons of the Grand Marnier. Beat the egg yolks with the sugar until lemon-coloured and thick. Stir in remaining Grand Marnier, orange juice and melted gelatine. Whip the egg whites until stiff. Fold this into the whipped cream and then fold into the soufflé mixture. Half-fill individual soufflé dishes or a 6-inch diameter soufflé dish with the mixture. Divide the diced sponge cake, soaked in Grand Marnier, among the individual dishes (or put into the large dish). Add the remaining soufflé mixture and freeze for 4 hours.

Dust with powdered chocolate or cocoa.

Cooks: *Alcoholic, but delicious!*

Hare and Venison Casserole

2 lbs venison or hare
1 oz flour
salt and pepper
2 oz butter
1 large onion

3 shallots
2 large carrots
1½ pints stock
3 cloves
bouquet garni

Cut meat into six portions. Roll in seasoned flour. Fry in butter for about 10 minutes to brown. Put into casserole and add sliced onion, shallots, carrots and stock, cloves and bouquet garni as required. Cover well and seal. Cook for one hour at 400°F (200°C, Gas 6), then reduce to 300°F, 150°C, Gas 2 for two hours.

Potted Shrimps

1 lb butter
½ lb shrimps
½ soupspoon tomato ketchup
nutmeg

ground black pepper
salt
a touch of Cayenne pepper

Warm the butter until very soft and mix in all the ingredients. Place into suitable sized moulds and allow 8 to 10 hours to set in a fridge. Serve on a leaf of lettuce and garnish with sliced lemon, quartered hard boiled eggs, a sprig of parsley and brown bread.

Cooks: *A very popular starter. May be served in ramekin dishes as an alternative to a mould, and garnished with a wedge of lemon and a little cress.*

Editor: *As one would expect, venison features strongly in the* Clans Cook Book. *The bulk of Scottish venison has been exported to Europe, especially Germany, in recent years. With the advent of commercial deer farming in Scotland, more of this excellent meat will be readily available for the home market.*

Borthwick

From Major The Borthwick of Borthwick, Baron of Borthwick, Heriot, Midlothian

Caledonian Cream

1 lb cottage cheese
2 large tablespoons Dundee marmalade
2 large tablespoons caster sugar

2 large tablespoons malt whisky or
  Glayva
2 tablespoons lemon juice

Mix all ingredients together, then beat well with a whisk. Place in individual glasses and freeze. Decorate with chopped nuts before serving.

Brandied Raspberries

12 oz granulated sugar
¼ pint water
1 lb frozen raspberries

1½ tablespoons arrowroot
2 tablespoons brandy

Dissolve sugar in water, and boil for 5 minutes. Stir in the raspberries and leave to defrost. Blend the arrowroot with a little water in a pan. Strain in the juice. Heat and stir until it boils and thickens. Add the brandy, pour over the raspberries and chill for a few hours.

Skirley

2 oz dripping or lard
1 onion

4 oz oatmeal
salt and pepper

Heat dripping until smoking hot, and fry onion till it becomes pale brown colour. Add oatmeal and salt and pepper, and mix well together. Continue cooking slowly with lid on for about 15 minutes. Serve hot with mashed potatoes.

Left front, Tarte à l'Oignon (MacKinnon); centre front, Dundarve Steak and Kidney Pudding (Macnaghten); centre left, Tomato Soup (Mackay); centre, Raised Game Pie (Carnegie); centre right, Mackerel Pâté (Sutherland); back left, Salmon Plait (Ogilvy); back right, Wheaten Loaf (Maclean).

Boyle

From Rear-Admiral The Earl of Glasgow, Fairlie, Ayrshire

Cold Tomato Soup

Serves 6

1 tin Italian tomatoes
½ pint cream
salt
chopped mint

Blend tomatoes to a purée. Fold in the cream by hand. Add a little salt and chopped mint. Keep back some mint and sprinkle on top before serving. Chill thoroughly and serve very cold.

Highland Flummery

Serves 4

1½ gills double cream
3 oz (by weight) heather honey
3 tablespoons whisky
½ teaspoon lemon juice
a sprinkle of medium oatmeal

Whip the cream until it is really stiff. Then gradually stir in the honey, melted but not heated. Add the whisky and lemon juice. Serve sprinkled with oatmeal which has been toasted in the oven for a minute or two. Be very careful as it burns easily.

Kelburn Mousse

Serves 6

1 15 oz tin Consommée
1 large Philadelphia cream cheese
  (half quantity of consommée)
2 teaspoons curry powder, or more
  to taste

Blend consommée and Philadelphia for a few minutes. Then add the curry powder and blend again, making sure that curry powder is well absorbed. Turn into a soufflé dish and put in fridge overnight. Sprinkle with chopped parsley before serving. In warm weather or a hot dining room the mousse melts rather quickly so it is best to keep it in fridge until as late as possible.

A very good starter.

Marinade for Venison

(to be used 24 hours before cooking joint)

¼ pint red wine
2 tablespoons salad oil
1 sliced shallot
2 bay leaves
freshly ground pepper
a few crushed juniper berries
  (if possible)
salt

Bring the ingredients to the boil and allow to cool. Pour over uncooked joint and turn frequently for 24 hours. Use the marinade in the gravy.

Brodie

From Ninian Brodie of Brodie, Brodie Castle, Forres

My kinswoman, Mrs Diana Brodie of Lethen, has given me this recipe for a sticky gingerbread. Diana is a splendid cook, but doesn't normally give recipes to anyone within a radius of 50 miles! She makes this exception for the Clan Brodie.

Sticky Gingerbread

3 teacups plain flour
1 small teaspoon baking soda
1 small teaspoon ground ginger
1 small teaspoon mixed spice
2 teacups sugar
8 oz margarine
8 oz treacle   bring to boil together
8 oz syrup
2 eggs
1 teacup boiling water

Sieve together dry ingredients. Add the boiled mixture, then the beaten eggs, and lastly the water. Beat well together. Pour into a greased and papered tin and bake in a moderate oven for about 1½ hours.

Cooks: *A tasty gingerbread: definitely for lovers of treacle. Gingerbread improves if stored wrapped in greaseproof paper and placed in an airtight tin for a few days before cutting.*

Opposite: Front, Gaspacho (Rollo); centre left, Dutch Pea Soup (Mackay); centre, Cold Tomato Soup (Boyle); right, Oxtail Soup (Wallace); back left, Sheriff Soup (Arbuthnott); centre back, Artichoke Soup (Macmillan).

Bruce

From The Earl of Elgin and Kincardine, Broomhall, Dunfermline

"Mother's Potted Sock" took its original form from father's survival recipes in 1941-42. The original was to collect milk (any old left-overs) and, when souring, tip into butter muslin a quantity which could be held in both cupped hands. Tie the muslin tightly and put the ball into the toe of an old sock. Hang sock in a cool, dark cupboard for a week, when a pleasant cheese will emerge.

From 18th-century records, I have learned that my family mainly kept the small black Angus cattle from Montrose, and one of those was slaughtered each week. Poultry was sent in from the tenant farmers in lieu of cash rental. Salt butter and cheese were regularly made and the doo' cot was culled once a month. Sea fish were abundant in the river Forth and in some winters the herring fleet anchored in the river at Charlestown harbour, near our home, and the catch was redd and smoked in the lime kilns there during the winter when the lime-working closed down.

Salt from the pans on the shore of the Forth was in great demand. An enormous ice-house was built, some quarter of a mile from Broomhall. A passage below the house enabled air to be drawn from the east to west, where a larder in tower form was constructed. The butchered carcases were hung up in permanently cool, airy conditions.

Maple Parfait

We make this delicious, simple ice cream with maple syrup from our Canadian friends.

4 eggs
8 fl oz maple syrup
1 pint whipped cream

Beat the eggs and add to very hot syrup (not boiling). Chill thoroughly and add to whipped cream. Beat well before freezing.

Mum's Potted Sock

Grate all odd ends of cheese into top of double boiler and add 1 tablespoon of cream and 2 of port or sherry, and a knob of butter. Melt down, stirring briskly, and pot in jars. Seal with melted butter.

Crème Brûlée

2½ pints single cream
12 egg yolks
2 level tablespoons caster sugar
vanilla essence

Heat the cream in the top of a double boiler until scalded. Beat the egg yolks with caster sugar until pale and creamy and add the hot cream and vanilla essence. Return to the double boiler and stir carefully over the heat until the cream thickens, taking care not to overheat, or it will curdle. Strain cream into a large, flattish dish and leave to cool.

Sieve caster sugar all over surface—quite thickly—and place under a hot grill, watching carefully, until the sugar has browned. Remove dish from heat and leave until the top is hard before refrigerating for at least 2-3 hours.

Editor: *Lord Elgin's family prefer their Crème Brûlée unbaked–this is a richer-than-most recipe. But if you prefer a more solid mixture, place your dish in a roasting tin of warm water and bake in a cool oven for 10 minutes. Then cool before adding the caster sugar.*

Buchan

From Captain David Buchan of Auchmacoy, Ellon, Aberdeenshire

Here are two rather special dishes which we as a family like a lot.

We have invented the name "spare orrels." Orrels is a local word for "bits of food left over." It's an excellent way of using up the more difficult bits of meat off a deer's ribs.

The limpets we discovered when picnicking on our lovely beaches in Buchan. It's not a recipe as such, but makes an entertaining side show at a picnic.

Baked Limpets

Ingredients
A good supply of fresh limpets.

Equipment needed
One large flat stone and a good sized bonfire of clean wood etc. from sea shore.

A bonfire should be built round the flat stone and while it is burning, the limpets should be collected. When the fire is really hot the burning wood should be removed from the top of the stone and the limpets placed on the stone, either shell side up or shell side down.
The limpets will cook in their own juice and the shells can easily be removed after about five minutes over a really hot fire. They should be eaten straight away while they are hot. The part of the limpet which clings to the rock can be tough and should not be eaten, but the whole of smaller limpets can be eaten.

Cooks: *Limpets can be removed from rocks with a wet knife and then boiled until the meat comes off the shell. However, this recipe provides a more unusual method of cooking for the adventurous!*

Spare Orrels

meat from small venison chops,
   which are difficult to butcher well,
   and likely to be untidy

1 onion, finely chopped
1 oz butter
olive oil
1 oz flour
¼ pint red wine
stock made from good carcases
salt and pepper
¼ pint double cream

Remove the meat from the bone and shape into tidy looking cutlets; lightly fry in a pan with the finely chopped onion in the butter and olive oil. Remove the meat from the pan and keep warm in a serving dish. Add the flour to the pan and stir well to remove lumps; add wine and stock and salt to taste, with freshly ground black pepper. Add the cream and a squeeze of lemon, and pour the sauce over the meat.

Editor: *With the price of all kinds of meat escalating, not just venison but a variety of "spare orrels" can be used in this way.*

Cameron

From Sir Donald Cameron of Lochiel, "MacDhomnuill Duibh," Achnacarry, Spean Bridge

---

Venison keeps very well in the deep freeze. My wife says that as venison fat congeals very quickly, you must serve it from the oven onto very hot plates. As it is a dry meat, you should take care to keep it moist. Add two glasses of red wine to the gravy, or serve with a Cumberland Sauce.

Kipper Pâté

½ lb filleted kippers
  (frozen ones will do)
½ oz butter for cooking fillets
1½ gills double cream (whipped)
1 teaspoon lemon juice
dash of Tabasco
Worcestershire sauce
paprika
black pepper—no salt
2 tablespoons melted butter

Using a small covered pan, cook the kippers gently in the butter until soft enough to work through a sieve or food mill. Fold the kipper purée into the whipped cream. Taste and season generously before stirring in the remaining butter, melted but not hot.
  Turn into a small bowl or individual ramekins and serve with toast.

Jubilee Venison

1 haunch from a fat juicy beast
3 tablespoons flour
1 tablespoon dry mustard
½ packet of cooking fat

Spread the mixed ingredients over the meat and wrap in tinfoil, so that top is covered twice.

Put in a hot oven (425°F, 210°C, Gas 7) for 45 minutes, a cooler oven (325°F, 160°C, Gas 3) for a further two hours. Uncover the top only, and cook for another 45 minutes. Serve quickly onto very hot plates.

Cooks: *To prepare the sealing paste (which is a variation of the traditional flour/water luting paste) melt the cooking fat then add the flour and mustard. This makes it easier for spreading over the meat.*

Traditionally, roast venison is served with clear gravy, redcurrant jelly and baked apples. Roast potatoes and fresh boiled vegetables are suitable accompaniments.

Cumberland Sauce

2 oranges
2 lemons
1 lb redcurrant jelly
8 fl oz port or red wine
2 heaped teaspoons arrowroot

Thinly peel one orange and one lemon. Remove pith and shred the peel finely. Bring a pan of water to the boil, add the shreds and boil for 3 minutes. Drain and cover with cold water for 1 minute, drain again and set aside. Squeeze and strain all the fruit juices into a pan, add the jelly and bring slowly to the boil. Simmer for 5 minutes, then add the port and bring the sauce back to the boil. Remove from the heat and stir in the arrowroot, mixed to a paste with cold water. Return to the heat and cook for 1 minute. Add the blanched peel and leave the sauce in a cool place for 24 hours.

Carnegie

From the Earl of Southesk, Kinnaird Castle, Brechin, Angus

The fish in "Croûte à la Findon" is named after a fishing village called Findon five miles south of Aberdeen, which is no longer active.

Raised Game Pie

Filling

Bone as many birds as you require (four is the usual number, for example 2 pigeons, 2 partridge) and farce them, using fresh pork or sausages. Braise or roast the birds, dice the meat and keep it warm.

Hot Water Crust Pastry

1½ level teaspoons salt
12 oz flour
¼ pt milk
4 oz lard or cooking fat

Add the salt to the flour. Bring the milk and lard to the boil, and stir in the flour. Knead well until smooth.

Take ¾ of the pastry (leave remainder in the pan and keep it warm). Line the raised mould with the pastry, and fill with chopped game. Using the remainder of the pastry make a lid, seal the edges, make a hole in the centre, and decorate with pastry leaves.
   Bake in a hot oven (425°F, 210°C, Gas 7) for 15-20 minutes.
   To serve hot—fill with stock made from game bones.
   To serve cold—dissolve 1 level teaspoon gelatine in 4 fl oz of game stock, and when almost cold, fill up the pie. Leave to set.

Rowan Pie

Take any cooked bird you have, preferably a boiled fowl. Shred the meat finely, and pour over a little of the stock in which the bird was cooked. Boil 2 oz macaroni and cut it in small pieces, flavoured with an onion, pepper and salt and half a pint of cream. Put all together in a pie dish and bake. When cold, garnish with aspic.

Green Butter

Blanch 1 handful of parsley. Take 1 oz butter, a little anchovy sauce, and a pinch of cayenne pepper. Put all through a hair sieve, shape into balls and serve.
    This should be the consistency of butter, and should spread easily on toast.

Cooks: *This would be an attractive accompaniment to fish dishes.*

Croûte á la Findon

Take the meat off two finnan haddocks, pound it and pass it through a wire sieve; mix with cream, pepper and salt. Put a little of the mixture on rounds of fried bread. Bake in sharp oven (425°F, 210°C, Gas 7) for 5 minutes.

Editor: *Findon Haddock is more commonly known as Finnan Haddock or even Finnan Haddie. Originally the fish was salted, dried, then smoked to withstand the journey from Aberdeen to Edinburgh. They are also excellent used in a mousse or pâté.*

Chisholm

From The Chisholm, "An Siosalach", Bury St Edmunds, Suffolk

My wife and four daughters are all excellent cooks, my son and I love eating. This is a Clan Chisholm collection which has our full approval.

Claire Mairi Hope's Marble Cake

From my third daughter, now Mrs John Turner

4 oz butter or margarine	pinch of salt
4 oz caster sugar	vanilla essence
2 eggs	2 tablespoons milk
5 oz self raising flour	

Cream the butter and sugar until light and fluffy, add whisked eggs a little at a time (if the mixture curdles, add a spoonful of flour and carry on beating). Add half the flour (sifted), then the other half with salt, vanilla essence and milk.

Divide into 3 bowls; add flavourings and colourings to taste. Place all three mixes into a greased and floured 7 inch baking tin. Bake for about 40 minutes at 375°F, 190°C, Gas 5.

Fudge Icing

2 oz butter	vanilla essence
2 tablespoons milk	8 oz icing sugar

Heat the butter and milk over a very low heat, and add the essence. Leave to cool. Sift the icing sugar into a bowl. Pour in the liquid and stir until smooth. Use when cold.

Sister Lucy's Salmon Mousse

8 oz cooked salmon (free from skin and bone)	salt and pepper
½ pint cold Béchamel sauce	½ oz gelatine (dissolved in 3 tablespoons stock)
¼ pint mayonnaise	3 oz double cream (lightly whipped)

Lightly oil a fish mould. Pound the salmon until smooth. Add the Béchamel sauce and the mayonnaise a little at a time. Season, then fold in gelatine and cream.

Turn into the prepared mould and leave to set.
Turn out, and coat with mayonnaise lightened with tomato juice. Garnish to taste.
Lucy is my youngest daughter.

Bessie MacAlpine's Chocolate Cake

Bessie is London Branch Secretary of the Clan Society.

5 oz self raising flour
3 oz drinking chocolate
4 oz butter
4 oz caster sugar

2 eggs
1 teaspoon vanilla essence
1 tablespoon milk
1 tablespoon hot water

Sift flour and drinking chocolate. Cream butter and sugar until fluffy. Add beaten eggs a little at a time, then the vanilla essence, flour and drinking chocolate, alternating with milk and hot water. Turn into an 8-inch deep cake tin lined with greaseproof paper. Bake in a moderate oven (350°F, 180°C, Gas 4) for about 40 minutes, or until firm to touch.
Serve plain or iced as desired.

Strawberry Shortcake

When I visited Nova Scotia with my wife, I was treated many times to this delicious Strawberry Shortcake. This is one of the recipes which my wife brought home.

8 oz self raising flour
pinch of salt
4 oz butter
2 oz caster sugar

2 eggs
fresh strawberries
7 oz carton double
    (or whipping) cream

Sift flour and salt into a bowl. Rub in butter until it resembles fine breadcrumbs. Mix in the sugar.
Make well in the centre and stir in the beaten eggs to bind mixture. Knead lightly on a floured surface then divide mixture and press into two greased 7-inch sandwich tins.
Bake at 350°F, 180°C, Gas 4 until just golden brown—approximately 35-40 minutes. Remove from tins and cool on wire tray.
When cool, spread the bottom half with half of the strawberries which have been crushed and mixed with a little caster sugar and whipped cream. Place the other shortcake on top and decorate with the remaining whipped cream and whole strawberries dusted with sugar.

Susan Catherine's Salmon Mousse

¾ salmon steak
2 tablespoons double cream
2 tablespoons sherry
1 oz butter

Béchamel Sauce:
    1 oz butter
    1 oz flour
    8 fl oz court bouillon

Court Bouillon:
    ¼ pint dry white wine
    ¼ pint water
    strip of lemon zest
    2 bay leaves
    1 small carrot
    1 small onion
    1 clove garlic
    1 clove
    salt and black peppercorns

Prepare court bouillon by combining above ingredients—in order to preserve the deep colour of the fish, this version of court bouillon is prepared without vinegar—then poach the salmon in the court bouillon until cooked (approximately 15 minutes). Allow to cool then remove skin and bone. Retain the liquid to make the sauce.

Prepare the Béchamel sauce by melting the butter in a saucepan then adding the flour to form a roux. Cook for 1-2 minutes then gradually add the court bouillon, beating well between each addition, in order to make a smooth sauce.

Pound the salmon and add to the sauce.

Cream the remaining 1 oz of butter and whip the cream. Fold the butter, cream and sherry into the salmon-sauce mixture.

Turn into a soufflé dish, smooth the surface then refrigerate until set.

Run over a thin layer of aspic. When this has set, garnish with a spray of chervil or dill. (Susan Catherine is my eldest daughter.)

Cooks: *This mousse, which contains no gelatine, is not suitable for unmoulding. Serve from soufflé dish or in individual ramekin dishes.*

Sister Catherine's Macaroni Salad

Sister Catherine Chisholm is a Sister of Charity, the daughter of Colin Chisholm, Chairman of the American Branch of the Clan Chisholm Society, and is Secretary of the Branch.

2 cups of short-cut macaroni
½ cup mayonnaise
1 tablespoon lemon juice
1 teaspoon salt
1 teaspoon sugar

¼ teaspoon celery seed
1 tomato (diced)
1 cup diced celery
3 tablespoons chopped pimento
2 tablespoons chopped green pepper

Cook the macaroni as directed. Mix the mayonnaise with the lemon juice, salt and sugar, combine with other ingredients. Serve on salad greens.

    Opposite: Altyre Chicken (Cumming).

Cochrane

From Major The Earl of Dundonald, Lochnell Castle, Ledaig, Argyll

My ancestor, Archibald, 9th Earl of Dundonald, was born in 1748; after a spell in the Royal Navy, he devoted his life to scientific pursuits. In February 1791, from Culross Abbey, he wrote three letters on the making of bread from potatoes, these letters being published in Edinburgh that year.

He said: "The discovery of a Method to make good Bread of the Potatoe, or its farina, has long been a desideratum, and the only thing wanting to render it the most useful of plants.

"The process of making a flour, or farina, from potatoes is similar to what has long been practised in the West Indies, by the negroes, in the preparation of the Cassava flour; viz., by grating down the root, and by subsequent and repeated washings with water, to free it from the juice, which is a strong poison. It is like-wise nearly the same as has been practised by families in the making starch from potatoes; for the meal or flour got from potatoes is a starch powder."

In his last letter, he said: "It will not be difficult to foresee the effect, that the more general cultivation of potatoes, especially by cottagers and manufacturers residing in the country, will have, in keeping down the price of provisions, adding to the general comfort of individuals, and in tending to the increase of population, which everywhere thrives best where food is to be had in abundance. An increase of population in these kingdoms, the natural consequence of plenty of food, is rendered the more necessary from the compact against us of the different branches of the Bourbon Family.

"Potatoe powder is very inflammable. When burning, it emits a smell similar to burning sugar, with an acid which sensibly affects the eyes, as in the case likewise with sugar. From these, and other circumstances, I am led to say that although sugar may not be made from potatoes, at least, in the present stage of our chemical knowledge, yet, it is my opinion that potatoe-flour may be used to good advantage in making ardent spirits, by mixing it with the proportion of malted grain, commonly used with unmalted grain at the distilleries. I think, also, that the spirit will be much purer than what is got from a mixture of malted and unmalted grain."

Potato Bread

1 lb strong plain flour
2 teaspoons caster sugar
½ oz fresh yeast *or*
   1½ teaspoons dried yeast
8 fl oz warm milk and water mixed
4 oz mashed potatoes
2 tablespoons oil
2 teaspoons salt

To prepare the yeast batter, mix together 4 oz flour, the sugar, the yeast and the liquid in a large bowl. Cover and set aside for approximately 20 minutes in a warm (but not hot) place. The mixture should then appear frothy.

Mix the potatoes, oil and salt into the batter, and add the remaining flour to make a firm dough. Turn the dough onto a lightly floured surface and knead for approximately 10 minutes until smooth and elastic. Shape the dough into a ball, place in an oiled polythene bag and leave to rise until doubled in size. Turn the risen dough onto a lightly floured surface, knock back and knead until the dough is firm once more. Divide into two pieces and shape to fit two well-greased (1 lb) loaf tins. Cover and prove.

Bake in the centre of a hot oven (450°F, 230°C, Gas 8) for about 25 minutes, until loaf is well risen with deep brown crust. Turn onto a wire rack, and cool.

Cooks: *The use of potato bread might awaken nostalgic memories in those who used it during the years of austerity. Potato flour is not commonly used in breadmaking nowadays, but leftover mashed potatoes (or dried instant potato) can be used to make this delicious bread.*

Editor: *The 9th Earl of Dundonald appears to have been a remarkably far-sighted man. Not only did he discover a process for making tar from pit coal, but he also lit his tar distilling works with the gas by-product.*

Cranston

From Lt. Colonel Cranstoun of that Ilk, Corehouse, Lanark

My wife is Italian, which might explain why so many of my favourite dishes come from that country. I should add that I am very proud of many Scottish dishes too!

As my wife has prepared these recipes many times, I feel she should add her own comments to them.

Ravioli Verdi

At a dinner party given by my sister in Vienna in 1954, she served, as a first course, "Ravioli verdi." This met with an enthusiastic welcome, especially by a smart Grenadier, then Deputy Commander of Vienna British Sector. This fact induced me to ask my sister for the recipe which, despite my lack of experience in cooking, I practised so assiduously that I was soon able to reduce the preparation time of seven hours to three quarters of an hour! Needless to say, "Ravioli verdi" is still one of the favoured dishes of my husband—the smart Scots Grenadier!

Mix 1½ lbs flour with 4 eggs, one or two teaspoons of salt, and enough warm water to get a firm paste. Using the "pasta-machine" or by hand, mould it into long thin strips, approximately 3 inches wide.

Filling
Lightly boil 1½ lbs spinach with salt; drip *very* well, chop finely and mix with; ½ lb cottage cheese (smooth, not granular), 2 eggs, 4 soupspoons of grated Parmesan cheese, crushed garlic (2 cloves), 1 stock cube dissolved in the minimum hot water, ½ teaspoon nutmeg (grated). This filling has to be firm. Put on the pasta-sheets, at a distance of approximately 3 inches from each other in little balls (with the help of a teaspoon). Fold the strips over the balls longitudinally, press with your hands all around each ball and cut little envelopes with a pasta stamp (half circles or squares). Put a teaspoon of salt and a teaspoon of oil into plenty boiling water; put the "ravioli" (previously placed on tea towels on big surfaces, like tables, trays etc.) into the water and bring back to the boil. Simmer for ¼ of an hour, drip thoroughly, build layers of "ravioli" in a wide, square Pyrex dish, alternating with flecks of butter and cream.

Instead of flecks of butter you may melt the butter with rosemary needles, bringing it to the boil, but *not* frying it. Serve very hot with much parmesan cheese on the top, and also on the table in the "formaggera" (parmesan cheese container).

Beef with Cinnamon

At a shooting party dinner in Lower Austria, we were very much taken by a dish of venison with cinnamon. On my return home I tried to reproduce it using beef, as I had been unable to obtain venison. My husband approved it unconditionally, especially if served with "salsa verde," an ancient recipe taken from my Piedmontese great aunt's hand-written recipe book.

Lightly fry 2 lbs stewing beef (in pieces) in hot butter and oil, in an open pressure cooker. Add 2 soupspoons of cream, ½ soup cube dissolved in a glass of hot water, 2 cloves garlic (crushed), salt and pepper. Put pressure cooker lid on and bring to the boil. Keep on a low heat for 30 minutes. Remove lid when cold, add one or two glasses of (possibly) Chianti wine, ½ teaspoon sugar, 1 soupspoon flour dissolved in hot water, 1 teaspoon of cinnamon (powder). Bring to the boil, cover with usual (not pressure cooker) lid, allow to simmer for 15 minutes. You can serve this dish either in a deep ashet, or separate the meat from the sauce (if necessary diluted with milk).

Salsa Verde

(Cold green sauce)

3 handfuls of fresh, very finely
  chopped parsley
1 oz white bread crumbs
2 fl oz olive oil (or other oil)

2 fl oz wine (or other) vinegar
3 crushed cloves of garlic
½ teaspoon dry mustard
salt and pepper to taste

Mix all the ingredients thoroughly together, and serve the following day.

Cumming

From Sir William Gordon Cumming, Altyre, Forres

Here are two dishes we favour very much. The Altyre chicken is an invention of Mrs D. Watt who has cooked for us for 17 years.

Altyre Chicken

Serves 8

1 boned medium chicken
1 boned pheasant
1 boned partridge
1 lb puff pastry
1 beaten egg

Stuffing
¼ lb minced pork
handful white breadcrumbs
a few mixed herbs
1 small grated onion
1 beaten egg
salt and pepper

Season each bird well with salt and pepper. Lay partridge on pheasant, and then pheasant on chicken. Mix minced pork, breadcrumbs, herbs, onion and beaten egg. Season well. Spread over the birds evenly. Roll chicken up carefully, keeping chicken shape as much as possible. Sew with bagging needle and thin string. Place in foil spread with butter. Season. Place in oven for approximately 1½ hours at 350°-375°F, 180°-190°C, Gas 4-5.

When cold, remove thread. Roll out half the pastry, and place the cold bird in the middle. Brush the edges well with beaten egg. Brush all over the other half of the pastry, and place over the bird, ensuring that all joins are sealed. Decorate with any left-over pastry. Brush all with remaining beaten egg, and place in oven for 1½ hours at 350°-375°F, 180°-190°C, Gas 4-5.

This dish is very easy to prepare if time is allowed for boning, as the first part of the preparation and cooking can be done in the morning.

Cooks: *An excellent recipe, which would be extremely suitable for any dinner party. If you can give your butcher sufficient warning, he may bone the birds for you, thereby vastly reducing the preparation time.*

Egg Mousse

Serves 4

4 hard-boiled eggs
1 dessertspoon Worcester sauce
1 dessertspoon anchovy sauce
1 tablespoon aspic jelly powder
   to ½ pint water
½ pint cream
salt and cayenne pepper

Sieve the egg yolks, add the sauces and ⅔ of the aspic jelly. Chop whites of egg very finely and add to mixture. Whip the cream, and add to mixture. Season to taste with salt and cayenne pepper.

Put into a soufflé dish. (If individual dishes are required, this mixture will fill eight ramekin dishes). When the mixture is set, decorate with cucumber or shrimps, then cover with the remaining jelly.

Editor: *This most unusual roast "en croute" is pictured on page 35. The variations in colour show the three birds used in the recipe which is much easier to produce than might be supposed, particularly if the birds are boned for you.*

Drummond

From the Earl of Perth, Stobhall, by Perth

My favourite recipes might fill this book. They all depend on the day—hot or cold; on what I've been doing—had exercise or sitting still; on who is sharing the meal.

My favourite meal uses the produce of Scotland; Arbroath Smokies, grouse and Perthshire raspberries. You'll be lucky to get the raspberries as late as August the twelfth, the first day you can eat a grouse, but try them with cream and sugar to taste, plus parkins, almost burnt brown.

For wines, go to France (the Auld Alliance). Start with a white Burgundy, go on to Claret and lastly a Moselle. And if you dance a reel after such a feast, it will do you no harm!

Parkins

2 oz granulated sugar	½ teaspoon cinnamon
2 oz lard	½ teaspoon mixed spice
3 oz syrup	1 teaspoon ginger
4 oz medium oatmeal	¾ teaspoon baking soda
4 oz plain flour	

Melt sugar, lard and syrup. Pour over dry ingredients previously mixed together. Roll pieces into balls, place half a blanched almond on top and bake in a moderate oven (350°F, 180°C, Gas 4) for 15-20 minutes. Cool slightly before removing from trays.

Cream Smokies

2 smokies
8 oz single cream

Slightly butter a shallow fireproof dish. Skin and bone the smokies and arrange in dish. Cover with cream. Place in a moderate oven (350°F, 180°C, Gas 4) for 10-15 minutes.

Roast Grouse

2 brace young grouse
2-3 oz butter
salt and pepper
4 slices toast or fried bread

fat streaky rashers of bacon
flour
dripping

Pluck, draw and truss the birds. If they are large, one bird may serve two people. Cream butter with salt and pepper and place a knob in the cavity of each bird.

Stand each bird on a piece of toast trimmed to size and put into a roasting tin. Cover birds with plenty of fat bacon (to prevent drying out during cooking). Dredge with flour and add a little dripping. Roast at 425°F, 210°C, Gas 7 for about ¾ hour, basting frequently, till tender.

Serve the grouse on the toast on which it has been cooked, garnished with watercress and served with fried crumbs.

Other accompaniments should be bread sauce, Baxter's Cranberry Jelly, straw potatoes, thin gravy made from pan drippings and a green salad.

(Recipe from Ena Baxter's Cookery Cards)

Brown Breadcrumbs

2 oz butter
1 teaspoon cooking oil

4 oz white breadcrumbs
seasoning

Heat the butter and oil in a frying pan. Add crumbs and cook over a steady heat till golden brown and crisp, turning all the time. Serve in an open dish, with roast grouse.

Editor: *As the Earl of Perth mentions, grouse shooting in Scotland begins on 12th August, "the glorious twelfth," the day on which the sporting guns take to the moors and the grouse take to the wing. The most common grouse is the Red Grouse which is to be found in its thousands in Great Britain (as well as a few in Eire). Probably the most spectacular of this family are the Capercailie, nearly the size of turkeys, which are brown with green, black, red and white plumage, and the Ptarmigan, which has brown and white plumage during the summer and pure white plumage during the winter.*

Members of the grouse family are also to be found in the United States, where there are also sage, sharp-tailed and blue-ruffed grouse. The prairie-chicken is also a grouse!

Elliot

From Sir Arthur Eliott of Stobs, Newcastleton, Roxburghshire

English Roast Beef

On a braw, bricht, moonlit nicht send several clansmen on horseback over the border into Cumberland to select a suitable beast. It is more economical and saves wear and tear on both horses and clansmen if several beasts are collected on the same sortie. Prepare as usual and invite to dinner any neighbouring Chief with whom you are not currently having a feud.

Chocolate Sauce

1 tablespoon butter
1 tablespoon granulated sugar
1 tablespoon cocoa powder
1 tablespoon golden syrup
2 tablespoons cold water

Melt all the ingredients together over a low heat. Do not allow the mixture to boil, or it may turn into toffee. Pour hot over ice cream.

Editor: *The recipe for the roast beef has not been tested, but the chocolate sauce is delicious. Incidentally, the two different spellings of the name of the Chief and of the Clan are correct.*

Erskine

From the Earl of Mar and Kellie, Claremont House, Alloa, Clackmannan

Ginger Cake

3 oz margarine
1 tablespoon syrup—make up
  to 12 oz with treacle
1 egg
4 oz caster sugar
½ pint warm water
12 oz plain flour
1 teaspoon ginger
pinch salt
1½ teaspoons baking soda

Grease a 9-inch square cake tin. Put margarine, syrup and treacle in a bowl over a pan of hot water. Mix together the egg and sugar, and beat into treacle mixture. Add warm water, then flour, ginger and salt. Leave the baking soda till the last. Stir well. Bake in a moderate oven, 350°F, 180°C, Gas 4 for 1 hour.

Cooks: *If a less "treacly" ginger cake is desired, adjust the ratio of syrup to treacle to achieve a blander flavour.*

Editor: *This recipe was appreciated so much by one of my guests that I was asked if a "doggie bag" could be supplied to take some home.*

Farquharson

Captain Alwyne Farquharson, "Mac Fionnlaidh," The Castle of Invercauld, Braemar, Aberdeenshire

---

My wife has a very direct approach to cuisine in which simplicity is the keynote. We use only the finest ingredients, grown, reared and wild from our estate—lovely salmon from the River Dee and a variety of game from the forest and moor. Lamb comes from our home farm as do the vegetables and soft fruit, so that all our menus are made up from those local ingredients.

Great emphasis is put on the butchering of meat, which is done here at Invercauld Castle so that when we present venison, for example, it has been prepared and hung in such a way that it is as tender as the most expensive of meat and consequently requires very little cooking. Everything is lightly cooked and seasoned with our own herbs; sauces are made only with vegetable oils and are always served separately. With the roast venison we serve our own rowan berry jelly and with minute steaks of venison we serve Béarnaise sauce (as with beef).

I remember one occasion on which an American guest found it impossible to believe that the juicy pink meat he was eating was venison. Knowing the red deer in his own country, he said it was nothing like the meat he was eating. "You must have a very special breed of Aberdeen Angus here," was his disbelieving reply. The answer was in the careful choosing of the beasts in their prime, gralloched on the hill, brought into the larder at once and hung for several days before being cut into saddle, haunches and shoulders. The saddle is roasted on the bone or grilled in cutlets. The haunches are butchered in pieces, removing all sinews since deer are jumping animals. The shoulders are mainly for stocks, casseroling and mincing.

Roast Venison

Venison is one of the most tender and delicious of meats for roasting, and very simple to cook.

Firstly we require best quality venison saddle or haunch. The beast should be hung for a period of 5-7 days so that the flesh is settled and firm.

Our butchering is done in the French method using mainly fingers to draw out each sinew and muscle.

Cooking
Baste venison on top of cooker to seal in juices, then put in a moderate oven (350°F, 180°C, Gas 4) allowing 5-7 minutes per lb.

Stuffed Shoulder of Venison

Bone the shoulder, and stuff as follows:

2 oz breadcrumbs
2 oz margarine
1 desertspoon finely chopped
   parsley
1 onion, finely chopped

2 teaspoons mixed herbs
pinch sage
½ cooking apple, chopped
   finely

Blend all the ingredients together and spread on the shoulder. Roll up and secure firmly with string. Cook in a moderate oven basting frequently, allowing 10-15 minutes per lb, according to taste.

Crowdie and Honey Tart

Pastry
8 oz flour
pinch salt
4 oz good quality soft margarine

1 tablespoon caster sugar,
   if desired
yolk of one egg and a little
   water

Sieve the flour and salt. Rub in the margarine until the mixture resembles breadcrumbs. Blend the egg yolk with water, (approximately 2 tablespoons), gradually add to flour mixture to make the dough into a rolling consistency. *Do not make the pastry too wet.* Roll on a lightly floured board and line the tin. Bake the pastry blind, lining with greaseproof paper and rice, which can be used over and over again. Bake in a hot oven (400°F, 200°C, Gas 6) for approximately 20 minutes, removing rice and greaseproof paper after 10 minutes.

Filling
3 tablespoons honey
6 oz Crowdie cheese, blended with

a little lemon juice and a
little milk or cream until smooth

Spread the pastry case with a little honey. Pour in the blended cheese mixture and decorate with chopped walnuts.

Editor: *If you are surprised to learn that Mrs Farquharson of Invercauld cooks the saddle for only 5 to 7 minutes per lb, remember that the meat is in its prime, well hung and just like fillet steak in texture and must not be overcooked. If your meat is not of this quality, then you would be well advised to add a few minutes per lb to your cooking time.*

Forbes

From Lord Forbes, Alford, Aberdeenshire

Apple and Cranberry Steamed Pudding

Make a pastry crust with 8 oz self raising flour, 4 oz margarine, a pinch of salt, and enough cold water to bind the pastry. Rub the fat into the salted flour till evenly crumbly.

Line a pudding basin with the pastry, leaving sufficient to form a "lid." Fill the basin with 1 lb peeled and sliced cooking apples alternating with 1 lb cranberries, sweetened with granulated sugar. Cover the fruit with the pastry "lid," damping round the edges to seal the "lid" to the pastry lining the bowl. Cover with greaseproof paper and a layer of tinfoil and tie these firmly in position with string.

Place the bowl in a pan of boiling water, with the water coming to two-thirds of the way up the bowl. Replace the lid on the pan, bring back to the boil and boil steadily for 1½-2 hours.

Loosen the pudding from the bowl by slipping a knife all round the inside, invert the bowl into a suitably sized, warmed dish and serve hot.

Cooks: *Although this recipe from Lord Forbes uses a shortcrust pastry, we would recommend that a suet crust pastry be used.*
8 oz flour
4 oz suet (chopped)
1 level teaspoon salt
2 level teaspoons baking powder
¼ pint water
Mix dry ingredients together. Add cold water and mix to an elastic consistency.

Italian Pheasant with Cream

1 roasting pheasant
fat bacon strips
salt and pepper
2 oz butter
1 small onion
½ pint double cream
1 tablespoon lemon juice

Tie the bacon across the breast of the bird and season the bird inside and out with salt and pepper. Melt the butter and fry the finely chopped onion until soft and golden. Pour over the bird and roast until just tender. Remove the bacon.

Pour the cream over the bird and continue cooking for 15 minutes, basting frequently. Just before serving, stir in the lemon juice then put the bird onto a serving dish. Stir the sauce well and add some blended flour to thicken it a little. Cook for a few minutes.

Either serve the pheasant whole, with the sauce separately, or joint the pheasant and place in a dish, pouring the sauce over the carved pieces of pheasant.

Equally good cold.

Editor: *The Italian Pheasant makes an excellent dinner party dish. I prefer to joint the bird in advance, keeping it in the warming drawer while I make the sauce.*

Fraser

From Brigadier Lord Lovat, "MacShimidh", Balblair, Beauly, Inverness-shire

I'm no expert on cooking food but my sister, Lady Veronica Maclean of Strachur, has included some of my favourite dishes in her book *Lady Maclean's Cook Book* [published by Collins].

Most of these come from Beaufort Castle, our family home, where we had the most wonderful cook in Miss Dorothy Fraser who came to our family as a kitchen-maid almost fifty years ago. We did a lot of entertaining at the Castle in the old days and needless to say Dorothy Fraser's reputation as a cook went far south of the Highland Line.

Cold Chicken Lovat

1 large boiling chicken with
  good breast
parsley
2 onions
1 pint cream

Boil the fowl for one hour with the parsley and onions. When cool, bone it and cut into pieces—not too big—using only white meat if possible. Put into an oven-proof dish with some of the reduced stock—a good cupful—cover and cook until tender, for about another hour, depending on the toughness of the fowl. Pour over one pint of cream and bake for half an hour more in a moderate oven (350°F, 180°C, Gas 4). Leave in a cool place until cold. The rest of the reduced stock will now have jellied into aspic: chop it up quite coarsely, and sprinkle over the top of the chicken. Serve in a 2½-inch deep entrée dish.

Opposite: clockwise from fruit: Banniskirk Flummery (Gunn); Raspberry Fool (Macmillan); Whisky Cream Pie (Grant); Crowdie and Honey Tart (Farquharson); Brandied Raspberries (Borthwick); centre, Flat Rock Pudding, (Urquhart).

Nun's Pudding

½ pint milk
4 egg yolks
4 leaves of gelatine

2 tablespoons apricot jam
2 teaspoons cinnamon
½ pint cream

Make the custard with the milk and 4 egg yolks. Add 4 leaves of melted gelatine. Pour into the dish into which it is going to be served and let set. Mix a dessertspoonful of water with the jam. Spread over custard. Sprinkle cinnamon over jam. Finish with thick layer of whipped cream.

Cooks: *4 leaves of gelatine is equal to ¾ oz powdered gelatine. To use leaf gelatine: wash in cold water, then soak in cold water until soft (15-20 minutes). Squeeze the softened gelatine lightly to extract surplus water and place in a bowl with 3 tablespoons water. Place bowl in a pan of hot water and heat, without boiling, until dissolved.*
    Leaf gelatine is normally used when a very clear jelly is required. Powdered gelatine would suffice in this recipe.

    There are two methods of dissolving powdered gelatine:

Method 1

Sprinkle the dry gelatine onto the hot water (⅛ pint for ½ or gelatine) and stir briskly for a few minutes. Set aside and continue with the recipe. You will find when the time comes for the gelatine to be used it will be a clear golden liquid.

Method 2

Soak gelatine in cold water–do this in a small bowl. Put bowl in pan of hot water–not boiling. Leave gelatine to dissolve and until it is a clear golden liquid.

Norwegian Cream

¼ oz gelatine
2 eggs, separated
4 oz caster sugar

½ teaspoon vanilla essence
2 tablespoons raspberry jam
¼ pint cream

Dissolve ¼ oz gelatine in ¾ teacupful (6 fl oz) cold water in a basin placed over a pan of hot water. Beat the egg yolks with 4 oz caster sugar and ½ teaspoon vanilla essence until thick and pale yellow. Beat in the cooled gelatine little by little until the mixture begins to stiffen. Now fold in, with a metal spoon, the stiffly-beaten egg whites.

Pour the mousse into a glass dish, and when cold cover with a thin layer of raspberry jam, which has been reduced by boiling with a little water and strained through a sieve. Cover with whipped cream.

Oxtail

1 oxtail	salt
2 oz cooking fat	paprika
2 onions	peppercorns
1 tablespoon flour	1 bay leaf
1 glass red wine	thyme, sage, parsley
water to cover	3 carrots

Cut the oxtail into joints and brown on all sides in the cooking fat. Add the sliced onions, flour and the wine and water. Stir in salt, pepper, bay leaf, and herbs. Cook in a casserole in a slow oven (300°F, 150°C, Gas 2) for about 3 hours or until the meat is tender. Add sliced carrots about half an hour before the meat is ready.

Editor: *Sir Fitzroy and Lady Maclean are the proprietors of The Creggans Inn in Strachur, Argyll where, as you would expect, many of the dishes featured in Lady Maclean's books can be found on the menu.*

Grant

From Lord Strathspey, West Wittering, Sussex

The Clan Grant Special

This is a cold vegetarian soup, where all natural vitamins etc., are preserved for your digestion.

Put a little water into a liquidiser and follow with some sliced tomatoes, a peeled and sliced apple or two, a handful of lettuce leaves or cabbage if no lettuce is available. Chop a smallish onion and throw that in. You can put in almost any vegetables you have to spare, but avoid potatoes. Celery and carrots are quite nice in moderation. Pour in about an eggcupful of olive oil, followed by seasoning as for Chief's Tomato Soup. Then liquidise the lot. Decant into glasses and put them in the refrigerator to cool off. Best eaten with a large teaspoon or a dessertspoon.

Chief's Tomato Soup

Take and peel by scalding, unless you finally sieve the result, a sufficient quantity of tomatoes and drop them after slicing up into a saucepan. Follow them with a cup or two of water to which a soup cube is added, or some stock instead, if you have it to spare.

Then look around and see what other surplus vegetables you have, say some boiled potatoes, cauliflower, lettuce, carrot, chopped celery or anything you care to taste which is to hand. Chopped onion is desirable for adding flavour.

Next add whatever seasoning you like. Salt and pepper are, of course, obligatory. Try a little Worcestershire sauce, cayenne or paprika. A teaspoon of sugar helps too. For heaven's sake use your imagination. Now, having inserted all the spare ingredients to hand that you fancy, boil it up, stirring with a wooden spoon occasionally until all is well cooked and soft, adding more liquid if too stiff. Then—and this is the technical and testing part—you can if you like press the whole through a fine sieve or pulp it in a mechanical liquidiser, in which event you may need to reheat the soup. Or you can miss out these two items and have it unpulped. Decant into soup bowls or plates and eat or drink it, preferably with a spoon. This is the time you learn of your mistakes but I have always enjoyed my mistakes. Very nourishing.

Cooks: *We tested the recipe using 1lb tomatoes and ½ pint water, which gave a good result.*

Gunn

From Iain Gunn of Banniskirk, Commander of Clan Gunn, London

My uncle, Dr William Gunn of Banniskirk, enjoyed entertaining his wide circle of friends at his house in Hampstead which is now, alas, demolished to make way for the new Royal Free Hospital where he was Consultant Physician for many years, and at Banniskirk House in Caithness where he spent his retirement. Like a sensible man, he persuaded his Irish cook in London to keep most of her recipes to herself, but he gave the recipe for a traditional Scottish pudding to my wife when we were staying with him at Banniskirk after our marriage.

As Banniskirk Flummery is very rich, my wife has invented a variation on the recipe, Whisky Cream Pie.

Banniskirk Flummery

1 pint double cream
1 teacup runny honey

4 tablespoons good whisky
a handful fine oatmeal

Whisk the cream, honey and whisky until thick, but not too stiff. Put the mixture in a glass dish, cover it and place it in a cool larder or the bottom of the fridge for at least one hour. Just before serving, sprinkle the surface with a handful of oatmeal.

Whisky Cream Pie

½ pint double cream
½ teacup runny honey
2 tablespoons good whisky
white of one egg

Flan Base
½ lb digestive biscuits
2 oz butter
1 tablespoon golden syrup

Melt butter and syrup in a saucepan. Crush the biscuits into fine crumbs and add to the pan. Coat the crumbs well with the mixture and then press into a flan tin. Whisk up the cream, honey and whisky until stiff; whisk the egg white until stiff and then fold it into the cream mixture. Spoon this into the crumb base and keep cool. Decorate with crystallized violets in the form of thistles, with a little thin angelica for stems.

Cooks: *It is advisable to prepare this pudding in a flan dish from which you can serve it at the table, as the biscuit crumb base is too crumbly to risk removing from the normal metal flan dish. It's a delicious pudding which will be well received.*

Haig

From The Earl Haig, Bemersyde, Melrose, Roxburghshire

In these hard days of dwindling salmon stocks, I look back with some nostalgia to the pre-war days when our Tweed salmon were plentiful and we had a splendid lady from Aberdeen, Mrs MacLeod, who left her granite house to come and cook for the family here during the holidays. Her salmon rissoles were not just fish cakes slung together with a bit of potato, but melted in the mouth.

Salmon Rissoles

1 lb fresh uncooked salmon
1½ cups of thick Béchamel sauce
   seasoned with salt and pepper and, if
   desired, a dash of paprika
chopped fresh dill or parsley
1 large egg
breadcrumbs (home made by baking bread
   in the oven until toasted hard and
   then crushed in a mill)
butter or margarine for frying
lemon wedges, cucumber

Prepare the thick Béchamel sauce, seasoned with salt and pepper, paprika, and fresh chopped dill or parsley.

Break the fresh salmon into a bowl, and whisk it until reduced to a mousse. Do not overbeat. Blend in the white Béchamel sauce and form into round cakes of approximately 2¾ inches by 1 inch thick.

Break the egg in a dish and with a fork stir it lightly until blended. Roll each fish rissole in the egg mixture and then coat with the breadcrumbs; fry them in a large skillet pan with sufficient butter or margarine until they turn golden on each side. Arrange on a hot plate, topped with lemon wedges and cucumber. Serve them warm with home-made sauce tartare or mayonnaise.

Hamilton

From the Duke of Hamilton, Hereditary Keeper of the Palace of Holyrood, Lennoxlove, Haddington

The melon starter is a particular favourite. My wife remembers it from her earliest days, being served at dinner parties by her mother. The recipe for the Avocado Pudding was given to my wife by the famous Portuguese pianist, Sergio Varella-Cid who discovered it when on tour in Brazil. This superb pianist was discovered by Arthur Rubenstein and first played in public at the age of five.

Melon Starter

1 melon
2 tablespoons mayonnaise
1 tablespoon sour cream or yoghurt
½ teaspoon curry powder

salt and pepper to taste
½ pint double cream, whipped
4 oz brown shrimps (or frozen if
  brown are unobtainable)

Using a scoop, make melon balls, saving the skin to use as a container.
   Mix the mayonnaise, sour cream (or yoghurt), curry powder and seasoning and fold into whipped cream. This should be done not more than half an hour before serving.
   Immediately before serving, add melon balls and brown shrimps to mixture (if frozen shrimps are used, they should be drained), and return to melon skin.

Avocado Pudding

2 ripe avocados
juice of a whole lemon
½ pint double cream, whipped
sugar to taste

Liquidise the flesh from the avocados with the lemon juice and sugar, fold in the whipped cream and chill for a few hours.
   This is a Brazilian recipe and tastes nicer than it sounds.

Hay

From the Earl of Erroll, Lord High Constable of Scotland, Stockbridge, Hants.

Here is a curious family recipe found in a manuscript book of *receipts* (the old word for recipes), called the *Household Book of Slains Castle*, written by Lady Erroll who married the twelfth Earl in 1674.

As for myself, I prefer the old-fashioned puddings like Bread and Butter Pudding!

Cold Snail Water

Take one gallon of new milk of a red cow—about one hundred great shell snails, wash them clean, crack them and throw away ye shells; a pint of great earth worms slit a long and clean washed—boyl these worms and snails in ye milk a bout half an hour, then pour them in a ordinary still and put to them of harts toung, alehooppe, cowslips of jerusalem and coltsfoot, of each a handful—cut ye erbs that they may ly well in ye still, and disstill them with a pritty hot fire, and now and then take of ye top of the still and stir it to ye bottom—let ye water drop on white shuger candy, two ounces to a quart—this will make a bout two quarts of water, its best to mingle it altogether—give ye child a bout eight or nine spoonfulls.

Bread and Butter Pudding

8 slices buttered white bread
2 oz sultanas
3 level tablespoons caster sugar

½ teaspoon cinnamon
2 eggs
1 pint vanilla flavoured milk

Cut the bread into 1-inch squares. Place them in a lightly buttered fireproof dish, with alternate layers of sultanas, sugar and cinnamon.

Mix eggs and milk. Pour over the bread and allow to soak for 5-10 minutes.

Bake in a pre-heated oven at 350°F, 180°C, Gas 4, for about 30 minutes or until set and lightly browned.

Keith

From the Earl of Kintore, Rickarton, Stonehaven

Kirsch Cream Cheese

1 large packet Philadelphia cream
  cheese
1 dessertspoon or so milk
2 or 3 tablespoons Kirsch
4 tablespoons granulated sugar

Use the milk to soften the cheese, and then add the Kirsch and sugar; beat it together thoroughly, till really well mixed, and put in the fridge for 2 to 3 hours, as this brings out the flavour. Excellent with nice big chunks of fresh pineapple or fruit salad.

Cooks: *A delicious alternative to cream– with an added kick!*

Editor: *If anyone has doubts about the authenticity of Viscount Arbuthnott's Sheriff Soup, these are dispelled by the Earl of Kintore who says that one of his fearless ancestors also took part—on the King's instruction—in the Sheriff stewing. Fortunately the Kirsch Cheese is undoubtedly a twentieth century dish.*

Leslie

From the Earl of Rothes, West Tytherley, Wiltshire

Super Scampi

Serves 4

2 oz butter
1 onion, chopped
8 oz mushrooms, peeled and sliced

6 tomatoes, peeled and quartered
1 lb peeled Scampi or large prawns

In a sauté pan heat the butter and lightly cook the onion, mushrooms, tomatoes and finally the Scampi. Serve immediately. It is important not to overcook this dish and to serve it very hot; the ingredients can be prepared beforehand as the cooking itself takes very little time.

Avocado Cheese

Serves 6

3 ripe avocados
juice of 1 large lemon
½ lb cream cheese

1 teaspoon finely grated onion
1 teaspoon salt
Worcester sauce to taste

Mash the pulp of the avocados, add the remaining ingredients and mix well. Chill thoroughly. Serve with hot toast or brown bread.

Cooks: *An easily prepared dish which may be served in the avocado skin, and garnished with a wedge of lemon. It will keep well for 2-3 days if stored in the refrigerator–the lemon juice prevents discolouration.*

Baked Chicken

Serves 4-6

1 chicken, jointed
4-6 oz mushrooms

4 rashers bacon
butter

Place the pieces of chicken on a large sheet of foil and add the peeled and chopped mushrooms and bacon. Add the butter and fold over the foil to make a sealed parcel. Bake for 1 hour at 350°F, 180°C, Gas 6. Serve hot, taking care to retain the juices.

Kipper Pâté

Serves 6-8

1 lb kipper fillets
4 oz butter
1 onion, finely chopped
juice of 1 lemon

3 tablespoons thick cream
freshly ground black pepper
chopped parsley and hard-boiled
  eggs to garnish

Poach kippers until tender, allow to cool and remove skin and bones. Sauté chopped onion in 1 oz butter until translucent. Place the kipper, onion and remaining ingredients in a blender and liquidise until smooth. Pour into individual ramekins and leave to set in the fridge. Remove one hour before serving, garnish with hard-boiled egg and chopped parsley. Serve with hot toast. (If served too cold much of the flavour will be lost).

Chocolate Cake

2 oz plain chocolate
2 oz water
3 eggs

4½ oz caster sugar
2½ oz plain flour
pinch of salt

Melt the chocolate in the water. Whisk the eggs and sugar until thick and creamy. Add the cooled chocolate to the egg mixture and fold in sieved flour and salt. Turn into a well greased tin and bake for 35 minutes at 350°F, 180°C, Gas 4.

McBain

From James McBain of McBain, Tuscon, Arizona, U.S.A.

Spareribs is a great favourite of mine, and of my father who was 22nd Chief. The Bar-B-Que sauce is normally made with commercially prepared sauces. However, one time we tried it using authentic Mexican spices. As a result we and our guests had to try to put a good face on what must have been the hottest food this side of hell! In retrospect, it was quite a comedy.

Carrot bread is an exquisitely light bread with a soft texture, but the taste of carrot does not come through. Our guests are very flattering in their praise of the carrot bread even though eyebrows are raised at first mention of it.

My wife Peggy (descended from the Forbes clan) is the guardian of our family recipes and supervisor of their preparation.

Spare Ribs in Bar-B-Que Sauce

3 lbs pork, lamb or beef
  spare ribs
½ cup bottled chilli sauce
½ cup bottled catsup (ketchup)
¼ cup vinegar
¼ cup molasses

Set oven at 450°F, 230°C, Gas 8. Cut ribs into serving pieces and bake in the oven for 30 to 45 minutes to brown and rend the fat. Remove from oven and drain off the fat. Reduce the oven temperature to 300°F, 150°C, Gas 2. Mix the chilli sauce, catsup, vinegar and molasses, stirring well. Pour on top of the spare ribs, cover with aluminium foil and return to oven. Cook for 2 hours until very tender.

Cooks: *Even using commercially prepared sauces, we decided that these ribs were a must for fire-eaters!! For catsup, substitute table sauce.*

62

Carrot Bread

2 eggs, lightly beaten
¾ cup vegetable oil
¾ cup sugar
1½ cups grated carrots

Mix the above ingredients together. To this mixture add the following:

1½ cups flour
1 teaspoon bicarbonate of soda
1 teaspoon cinnamon
½ teaspoon salt
½ cup chopped nuts

Bake in a greased loaf pan at 350°F, 180°C, Gas 6 for 75 minutes.

Cooks: *It may not help you see in the dark, but it is a delicious, moist teabread.*

Editor: *Lady MacDonald of Skye tells me she produces a superb carrot gâteau in her hotel there but doesn't use carrot in the name as it tends to be off-putting.*

Kinloch Gâteau (Macdonald).

Scotland produces the very finest of foods.   65

Macdonald

From Lord MacDonald, Armadale, Isle of Skye

At our hotel you will find "Kinloch Gâteau" on the menu. This, in fact, is Carrot Cake but my wife insists that if it is called Carrot Cake, no one will eat it. It really is delicious.

Kinloch Gâteau (Carrot Cake)

The quantities given make a huge cake, so if you prefer something smaller, then simply halve the quantities.

18 fl oz (nearly 1 pint) vegetable oil (e.g. sunflower)
1½ lbs caster sugar
6 eggs
¾ lb sieved plain flour

1½ teaspoons baking powder
1½ teaspoons bicarbonate of soda
1½ teaspoons cinnamon
½ teaspoon salt
15 oz grated raw carrot

Beat together the oil and caster sugar, gradually adding the eggs one at a time. Beat well. Add the sieved dry ingredients then the grated raw carrot. Mix all thoroughly.

Put into three well-greased and floured cake tins and bake in a moderate oven (around 350°F, 180°C, Gas 4) for one hour.

Fill and cover the cake with this butter cream—it completes this heavenly pud!:

Beat thoroughly ¾ lb butter and ¾ lb cream cheese (e.g. Philadephia), and gradually add 1 packet icing sugar and 1 teaspoon vanilla essence.

Curried Apple Soup

Many people are diet conscious these days. As this soup is very low in calories, it makes a very good starter to a rather rich dinner.

1 oz butter (or margarine)
2 large onions, peeled and chopped
1 dessertspoon curry powder
4 apples—2 cooking and 2 dessert, peeled, cored and chopped

1½ pints good chicken stock (or 2 chicken stock cubes dissolved in water)
salt and pepper

Melt the butter, add the onion and cook until transparent. Add the curry powder and cook gently for a minute or two. Add the chopped apple and stock and simmer gently for 10-15 minutes. Cool, liquidise and season to taste.

This soup will keep for three days in the fridge, or can be frozen. It is very good served hot or cold.

Editor: *Lord and Lady Macdonald own the Kinloch Lodge Hotel in Sleat, hence the name "Kinloch Gâteau."*

Macdonald of Clanranald

From Ranald Macdonald, The Captain of Clanranald "Mac Mhic Ailein"
Smarden, Kent

Champignons à La Normande

Serves 4

6 oz Normandy butter
2 small cloves garlic
¾ level teaspoon salt
¾ oz onion, grated
juice and rind of 1 small lemon
5 turns of peppermill
nutmeg
chopped parsley
2 oz fresh breadcrumbs
1 lb button mushrooms
2 oz clarified butter

Beat butter until soft, add rest of ingredients, apart from mushrooms and clarified butter, roll in foil in sausage shape and put in fridge to cool. Then cut into small slices. Fry mushrooms lightly in clarified butter, put in an ovenproof dish, cover with sliced mixture and put under grill until golden.

To clarify butter
Melt butter, filter through a piece of muslin (or use a conical sieve and some kitchen paper). This removes the milk solids and salt from the butter and enables it to be heated to a higher temperature.

Cooks: *This could be a lovely accompaniment to chicken or pork.*

MacDougall

From Madam MacDougall of MacDougall, Dunollie Castle, Oban

We used to love going into the big kitchen to watch our cook, Lizzie MacNiven—later followed by her sister Polly—make scones, pancakes and oatcakes on an iron girdle on the big, black iron coal-fired range, let into the arch of the early seventeenth-century fireplace. The range was black-leaded and its steel hinges kept beautifully polished. The heat of the oven was regulated by mysterious things called dampers. The floor was great slabs of stone with a large, scrubbed wood table down the middle and the whole was presided over by cook who was of ample proportions and enveloped in a clean white apron with a bib.

In front of the range lay an assortment of cats and dogs, large and small, round which cook picked her way.

Pancakes were great favourites and it was always supposed that if in winter you added a little snow to the mixture, they were lighter and more delicious. The scones were always mixed with buttermilk, left after the butter had been made from the milk of our own Jersey cows.

The recipe for the Black Bun was given to me over 50 years ago when I visited old Miss Colina MacDougall at New Year.

Drop Scones (or Pancake Scones)

1 cup self raising flour
½ cup sugar
1 egg
salt
½ oz melted butter
milk to mix to a dropping consistency

Mix ingredients together. Drop spoonfuls on a hot greased girdle (or thick frying pan). When bubbles appear on the surface, and burst, turn the pancakes over and cook for a few minutes longer. Place on a clean tea-towel on a rack, and cover with another tea-towel.

Black Bun

Pastry
1 lb flour
6 oz butter
½ teaspoon baking powder

Mix into a firm paste with water. Roll into a thin sheet. Grease the inside of a cake tin and line it neatly with the paste, reserving a piece for the top.

Filling
1 lb flour
2 lbs raisins
¼ orange peel
½ oz ground ginger
½ oz Jamaica peppers (allspice)
½ lb sugar

2 lb currants
¼ lb almonds
½ oz cinnamon
½ teaspoon black pepper
1 small teaspoon bicarbonate of soda
1 teaspoon cream of tartar
a good breakfast cup of milk

Mix thoroughly together and press the mixture into the paste-lined tin. Make it flat on the top, wet the edges of the paste and place the lid of paste on top. Prick all over with a fork, brush with white of egg, and bake in a moderate oven (350°F, 180°C, Gas 4) for 3 hours.

Cooks: *This cake should be made a few weeks before required in order to allow it to mature and mellow before eating.*

Chestnut Stew

1 lb chestnuts
1 large onion
3 carrots
pepper and salt

1 tablespoon flour
1 lb steak
1 pint stock (or 1 beef cube,
    1 pint hot water)

Place chestnuts in water and boil for 10 minutes. Cut up onions and carrots and fry until nicely brown. Mix flour, salt and pepper and roll steak in it, and fry with the vegetables for a few minutes only. Place in casserole and cover with stock. Add skinned chestnuts. Cover tightly and cook in a moderate oven (350°F, 180°C, Gas 4) for 2 hours.

Cooks: *If you have difficulty obtaining fresh chestnuts, ask for dried ones in a Health Food Store. Soak them overnight then follow recipe.*

Editor: *In Scotland, a girdle was not something one wore to hide the excesses of overeating, but what is known in English as a griddle. Around 18 inches to 2 feet in diameter, they were usually of black cast iron and very heavy.*

Mackay

From Lord Reay, Kasteel Ophemert, Ophemert, Gelderland, Holland

---

The family home of the Chiefs of the Clan Mackay has been here in Ophemert, Holland, for the past hundred years, the title of Lord Reay at that time going over to the Dutch branch of the family. This branch had established itself in Holland in the 17th century when the younger son of the 2nd Lord Reay went over to command the First Regiment of the Scots Brigade. His descendants then established themselves in Holland until my great uncle inherited the title and assumed British nationality. However, we continue to retain Dutch property.

Incidentally, I also have the title Baron Mackay van Ophemert en Zennewijnen, on the Dutch side!

Tomato Soup

12/14 tomatoes
2 cloves garlic
1 dessertspoon sugar
salt and black pepper
¾ lb peeled prawns or shrimps
butter
1 teaspoon olive oil
brandy
½ pint cream

Peel tomatoes, put in a saucepan with ½ cup of water, add crushed garlic, sugar, salt and pepper. Cook for ten minutes until the tomatoes are a rough mash. Meanwhile melt the butter and heat with oil, throw in shrimps, bring quickly to boil, add brandy and light it. All this should be done quickly in order that the shrimps do not overcook. Add to the tomatoes and mix in cream. Serve immediately.

Dutch Pea Soup or Erwtensoep

1 lb of fresh bacon (smoked if
   frankfurters are used—see below)
2 quarts water
1 pint shelled or frozen peas
1 sprig mint
2 sprigs parsley
1 oz butter
1 oz flour
salt, pepper to taste
20 baby carrots or 2 large carrots
   (sliced lengthways)—simmer till tender
5-6 medium leeks chopped finely and
   simmered till tender
1½ lbs smoked red sausage (frankfurters
   are a poor but possible substitute)
½ lemon

Make the stock by boiling the bacon in water. Remove the bacon and chop. Add the peas and herbs to the stock, and cook until tender. Strain the peas (keeping the water) and rub them through a nylon sieve. Melt butter in clean pan, mix in flour, pour on stock and stir until boiling. Whisk in pea purée and season. Simmer this for a few moments and then add the cooked carrots and leeks and the sausage (which should be chopped into 1½-inch lengths). Simmer until the sausage is cooked (15 minutes). Finish with a little cream and juice of ½ a lemon. A good loaf of bread should be offered with this dish.

Cooks: *A delicious main meal soup, probably more suited to a knife and fork than a soup spoon.*

Editor: *The "Reay country" in the North-East of Scotland, including the Clan seat of the House of Tongue in Sutherland, was sold to the House of Sutherland in 1829.*
   Like the Arbuthnotts, the Mackays believe in soup with body to it. Lady Reay tells me that the Dutch Pea Soup is a main course. No sweet has been suggested as the family prefer to finish a meal with cheese.

Mackenzie

From the Earl of Cromartie, Castle Leod, Strathpeffer, Ross-shire

---

The Worcesterberries used in the Pavlova are found in abundance at Castle Leod, but any other berry fruit can be used.

Worcesterberry Pavlova

Make pavlova and fill with purée of Worcesterberries (cooked in a very little water with sugar to taste and squeeze of lemon) immediately before serving. Running cream and sugar are tasty accompaniments.

This can be made with any other berry fruit.

Pavlova
4 egg whites
8 oz caster sugar
½ teaspoon vanilla essence
½ teaspoon vinegar
1½ teaspoons cornflour

Draw a 7-inch circle on greaseproof paper or rice paper. Wet the greaseproof paper and place on a baking tray.

Beat the egg whites until soft peaks form. Beat in the sugar gradually to form stiff peaks. Mix the vanilla essence, vinegar and cornflour. Fold this into the mixture. Spread some of the mixture over the paper circle. Put the remainder of the mixture into a piping bag with a large star nozzle and pipe a line round the top of the circle to form sides. Pipe four stars round the top.

Bake in the oven at 300°F, 150°C, Gas 1-2, for about 1 hour, until firm. Leave to cool, then carefully remove paper. (If rice paper was used, leave this on.)

Arbroath Smokie Cocottes

2 smokies, flaked
½ lb firm tomatoes—skinned, deseeded
   and chopped

Mix with ¼ pint cream and season. Serve hot in individual cocottes with homemade wholemeal bread and butter.

Cooks: *As smokies are already cooked, just place cocottes in a hot oven until heated through.*

Venison

Marinade a roasting joint for 24 hours in a mixture of wine vinegar, wine or cider, olive oil (plenty), seasonings, crushed garlic, and herbs, turning several times. Under-roast (15 minutes per lb) in a hot oven (425°F, 210°C, Gas 7) until meat is pinky-brown, in the marinade and with the meat covered in butter papers. When cool, carve in slices and arrange on a flat ovenproof dish. Cover with sauce made from pan scrapings, a little flour, red wine and rowan jelly (or redcurrant jelly). Cover entirely with foil and heat gently for ½ hour. Serve with mashed potatoes, and a green vegetable (spinach or whole green beans).

Editor: *Worcesterberries were unknown to me and to many expert cooks and cookery writers I consulted. However Mary Meredith, Cookery Editor of* Woman and Home *magazine, served an interesting sweet at lunch one day and when I asked the name of the fruit in it, she said she didn't know the exact name, but an old chap who was a dry-stane dyker working at her sister's cottage at Snaigo Estate, near Dunkeld in Perthshire, called them "goozleberries." She described them as a cross between a gooseberry and a blackcurrant. I then asked the Earl of Cromartie to describe a Worcesterberry and he said it was a cross between a gooseberry and a blackcurrant! He brought the bushes from Tarbat House in Easter Ross, his mother's former home, and transplanted them to Castle Leod, Strathpeffer.*

MacKinnon

From Neil MacKinnon of MacKinnon, Nailsbourne, Somerset

We have no particularly Scottish or MacKinnon recipes in the family, other than in two old recipe books dated 1625 and 1710. They are inclined to start with "Take six chickens . . ." and go on to say "three tongues etc. for the gravy." These books came to me through my grandmother, who was a daughter of Admiral Hood.

My mother was Danish, so the Danish sweet Rødgrød is a great favourite with the family. My wife makes it in British fashion with cornflour instead of the traditional potato flour.

Ham Steaks

1 oz butter
4 ham/gammon steaks ½-inch thick
  (6 oz each)
1 tablespoon flour
½ pint milk
1 teaspoon Worcester sauce
paprika
2 tomatoes
parsley

Melt the butter in a frying pan, and fry the ham on both sides to seal in the juices. Put in an ovenproof dish. Stir flour into the butter, cook for 1 minute, and then add the milk gradually, then the Worcester sauce and paprika. Stir till thick. Pour over the ham and cook in a slow oven (300°F, 150°C, Gas 2) for 20 minutes. Garnish with tomatoes and parsley.

Rodgrod

"Grød" (stewed fruit) made with a mixture of raspberries and redcurrants, or rhubarb or blackcurrants, etc.

1 lb fruit
1 level tablespoon cornflour
1 pint water
3-4 tablespoons sugar

Cook the unwashed (but peeled or "strung") fruit in water until soft. Strain through a Mouli sieve. Add the cornflour (mixed with a little water) and bring to boil. Add sugar and boil for 3 minutes, *stirring all the time.* Pour into a dish, sprinkle with caster sugar and decorate with almonds if liked. Cool. Serve with cream.

Tarte à l'Oignon

Peel and chop 3 or 4 onions. Put them in frying pan with 1½ tablespoons oil, 1 tablespoon butter and a little salt and pepper. Cook very slowly, stirring occasionally, until soft and transparent. Line the flan tin (7 or 8-inch) with shortcrust pastry. Mix the soft onions with a breakfast cup of cream, or top of milk, beaten with 3 eggs and salt and pepper. Pour into pastry case and cook for about 35 minutes, in a moderate oven 350°F, 180°C, Gas 4 until the mixture is set.

Editor: *See the story of potato flour under the Dundonald family entry. The Earl of Southesk tells me that Rødgrød was also a very popular dish with his mother-in-law, The Princess Royal, Duchess of Fife.*

Mackintosh

From Lieutenant Commander The Mackintosh of Mackintosh, Moy Hall, Tomatin, Inverness-shire

Here is one of my favourite recipes and one which my wife finds useful on a busy day.

Nutty Chicken

Serves 4

1 (10½ oz) can condensed mushroom soup
½ pint milk
8 oz cooked chicken (chopped)
5 oz long grain rice (cooked)
4 oz mushrooms (chopped)

2 oz peanuts (shelled)
3 rashers streaky bacon
 (finely chopped)
2 oz Cheddar cheese (grated)

Preheat the oven to 400°F, 200°C, Gas 6. Mix the soup with the milk in a large bowl. Stir in the chicken, rice and mushrooms, and turn into a 1½-pint pie dish. Coarsely chop the nuts and mix with the bacon and grated cheese, sprinkle over the pie.
   Bake the pie for 25 minutes, until the topping is golden brown.

Editor: *This is one of the excellent recipes given in the* Pennywise Cook Book *published by the Milk Marketing Board.*

MacLean

From Lord MacLean of Duart and Morvern, Duart Castle, Isle of Mull

---

Crunchies

4 oz margarine
5 oz porridge oats
3 oz sugar
pinch salt
(lemon juice)

Melt the margarine, without letting it boil, add to oats and sugar, etc., and mix well. Grease a baking sheet and spread mixture onto it. Bake at 375°F, 190°C, Gas 5 for approximately 15 minutes, until pale golden colour.

Spicy Crumb Cake

1 lb self raising flour
pinch salt
8 oz margarine
6 oz sugar

approximately 4 tablespoons jam
1 heaped tablespoon coffee powder
2 level teaspoons mixed spice

Sift the flour and salt, rub in margarine, add 4 oz of the sugar. Divide in half. Form one half into a shortbread dough, press into 2 greased sandwich tins. Cover with a layer of jam. To the other half add coffee, spice and remaining sugar. Rub until like breadcrumbs in consistency. Pile on top of jam base. Bake at 300°F, 150°C, Gas 2 for approximately 30 minutes, until golden brown. While still warm, cut and sprinkle generously with sugar and spice.

Wheaten Loaf

10 oz wheaten flour
6 oz plain flour
1 teaspoon salt

1 teaspoon bicarbonate of soda
2 oz margarine
¾ pint buttermilk

Mix the flour, salt and soda and then rub in the margarine. Add the buttermilk. Turn into a floured loaf tin and bake in a hot oven (375°-400°F, 190°-200°C, Gas 5-6) for ½ to 1 hour, until firm in the centre.

Lady Mac's Special Cake

4 oz margarine
¾ lb-1 lb cakecrumbs
2 heaped teaspoons baking powder
1 heaped teaspoon cocoa
2 heaped teaspoons mixed spice

1 cup sugar
2 eggs
milk
jam
mixed fruit

Melt the margarine, add to dry ingredients with beaten eggs and enough milk to make a moist mixture. Pour into a large greased (deep) tin and bake at 300°F, 150°C, Gas 2 for 1½-2 hours. When cool, turn out of the tin and spread warmed jam over the top. Old scones and spongecakes are particularly successful in this cake.

Economical Shortbread

1 lb self-raising flour
salt

8 oz margarine
4 oz sugar

Sift the flour and salt together, rub in margarine and sugar, kneading thoroughly until a pliable dough is formed. Press into a large well-greased baking tray, roll to flatten the surface, and prick all over with a fork. Bake at 300°F, 150°C, Gas 2, for 30-35 minutes.

Tea Loaf

$1\frac{1}{2}$ lb mixed dried fruit
$\frac{1}{2}$ lb moist brown sugar
$\frac{1}{2}$-$\frac{3}{4}$ pint strong cold tea
2 eggs
1 lb self raising flour

Mix the fruit and sugar with the tea and leave for a few minutes. Beat in the eggs and then stir in the flour. Turn into 2 greased and floured $1\frac{1}{2}$ lb loaf-tins and bake for two hours until firm in the centre.

Brownies

4 oz margarine
8 oz sugar
vanilla essence
2 eggs
3 oz plain flour
$1\frac{1}{2}$ oz cocoa
$\frac{1}{2}$ teaspoon baking powder

For the coffee frosting:
2 oz margarine
2 tablespoons coffee
1 tablespoon milk
8 oz icing sugar

Cream the margarine, sugar and essence until fluffy, add eggs and beat well. Stir in the dry ingredients. Place in a greased 7 x 11-inch tin and bake at 325°F, 170°C, Gas 3 for 25-30 minutes. Cut into fingers while still warm.

To make the frosting: melt margarine in pan, add coffee—boil steadily for 2 minutes. Quickly blend in the icing sugar and milk and then beat until the frosting is cold, and stiff enough to spread. Cover the tops of brownies with the frosting and decorate with chocolate dragees.

Editor: *There is a very popular tea-room at Duart Castle (which is open to the public), where visitors will find most of Lady MacLean's recipes on the menu.*

Beef with Cinnamon (Cranston).   82

MacLennan

From Ronald G. Maclennan of Maclennan, Clachan, Lochbroom, by Ullapool

Two of our favourite family recipes are Fillet of Beef Stroganoff and an "after dinner with coffee" treat called Helva. I'm told it's from the Middle East and has several names and several variations. My wife always makes it when the family requires cheering up.

Beef Stroganoff

Serves 2

12 oz long grain rice
1 oz butter
2 oz mushrooms
2 oz onions
1 clove garlic (optional)
3 small capers

1 chopped gherkin
12 oz fillet steak
salt and pepper
1 measure brandy
4 oz cream

Boil the rice in salted water until cooked. Melt butter in frying pan, mix in mushrooms, onions, garlic, capers and gherkin. Cut the fillet steak into strips, finger length, and add to the sauce. Cook slowly for 5 minutes, and season.

Add the brandy to the sauce while cooking, and finish off with cream. Leave to reduce for 3 minutes. Drain the rice and dry it off. Make a well in centre of the rice on a plate and add the stroganoff.

Helva

6 oz granulated sugar
4 oz butter
4 oz semolina

2 oz ground almonds
powdered cinnamon

Melt the sugar slowly in $\frac{1}{4}$ pint of water, bring to the boil and simmer for 10 minutes. Let the syrup cool while melting the butter. Add the semolina to butter and stir gently over a low heat for 5 minutes or so until the semolina is just colouring. Stir in the ground almonds; cook for 2 minutes, then stir in the syrup. Continue stirring until the mixture becomes thick (2-3 minutes). Pour onto a board which has been dusted with cinnamon, sprinkle cinnamon on top and mark into squares.

MacLeod

From John MacLeod of MacLeod, Dunvegan Castle, Isle of Skye

Although my grandmother, Dame Flora MacLeod of MacLeod had a very healthy appetite, she was totally disinterested in food, never cooked and couldn't even boil an egg! But if there was a dish one could say she favoured above others, it would be Scotch Eggs.

However, my Bulgarian wife loves cooking and I, as well as our two children, love eating her food. Our three family recipes all originate in Bulgaria.

Scotch Eggs

4 eggs, hard-boiled
1 oz seasoned flour
8 oz pork sausagemeat

1 beaten egg
breadcrumbs for coating
oil for deep frying

Remove the shell from the eggs, then toss eggs in seasoned flour. Divide the sausagemeat into 4 equal-sized pieces. On a floured board, roll each piece to form a circle, then mould round the eggs, taking care to completely cover them. Coat in beaten egg and breadcrumbs.

Deep fry in oil, which has been pre-heated to a temperature of 340°F, 170°C, for approximately 8 minutes by which time the Scotch Eggs should be crisp and lightly browned. Drain well on kitchen paper. Serve hot or cold.

Tarator

Serves 6

1 clove garlic (crushed)
60 g crushed walnuts
dill, salt and pepper

450 g natural yoghurt
1 small cucumber
1 tablespoon olive oil

Crush together the garlic, walnuts and seasoning; stir into the yoghurt. Add the finely chopped cucumber, dill, olive oil and seasoning. Serve chilled with ice cubes.

Peppers Stuffed with Veal

8 large peppers
salt
oil for frying
2 onions
paprika, black pepper and parsley
150 g rice

750 g minced veal
200 g tomatoes
1½ cups of natural yoghurt
   (2 x 140 ml cartons)
1 tablespoon flour
3 eggs

Wash the peppers and cut off the tops; remove the stalks and the seeds, salt the insides slightly. In a frying pan lightly brown the finely chopped onions. Add the paprika, black pepper and rice; stir and pour on half a cup of hot water.

Add the meat, the peeled and chopped tomatoes and the parsley, then simmer for ten minutes.

Fill the peppers with the stuffing and sprinkle flour on top of the filling. Arrange them in a deep casserole. Pour 1½ cups of hot water into the dish and cook in a moderately hot oven for about 40 minutes.

Beat the yoghurt with the flour and eggs, add some of the sauce from the casserole, pour the sauce over the peppers and put them in the oven for a further ten minutes.

Serve hot with this tasty sauce: heat 4 oz salted butter until boiling, add a teaspoon of paprika, stir quickly and remove from heat. Serve immediately.

Easy Apple Cake

1 cup flour
1 cup semolina
1 cup sugar
1½ teaspoons baking powder

8 small or 6 large cooking apples
3 tablespoons chopped nuts
cinnamon
4 oz butter

Mix the dry ingredients. Peel and grate the apples and divide into three equal amounts. Grease a 7-inch cake tin and evenly spread one cupful of the dry mixture on the bottom; on top of this spread one third of the apples; sprinkle with 1 tablespoon of nuts and a little cinnamon. Put pieces of butter on to this. Repeat the layers, finishing with apples on top. Bake in a moderate oven (350°F, 180°C, Gas 4) until cooked—approximately one hour.

Macmillan

From General Sir Gordon MacMillan of MacMillan, Langbank, Renfrewshire

Artichoke Soup

Serves 5-6

1 lb globe artichokes
1 large onion
butter

salt and pepper
1 pint chicken stock
1 pint milk

Soak the artichokes and scrub very well. Cut any large pieces to ensure even size. Skin and slice the onion and sauté in butter until soft. Add the artichokes, salt and pepper and stock. Simmer with the lid on until tender. Cool. Liquidise and rub through a sieve with a ladle. Return to saucepan and add the milk. Adjust seasoning.
   Serve hot sprinkled with chopped parsley.

Cooks: *A delicious soup, if you are ever in the lucky position of having a glut of globe artichokes! Tinned artichokes may be substituted—one 15 oz tin should suffice.*

Leeks au Gratin

2 leeks per person
cheese sauce (about ¼ pint per person)
streaky bacon

Wash the leeks well and soak, then cook gently until just soft. Make a cheese sauce. Wrap each leek in a rasher of bacon and set in a shallow ovenproof dish. When all are assembled, pour over the cheese sauce. Top with grated cheese. Brown in the oven or under a grill. This is a good dish to prepare in advance.

Victoria Sandwich

For a 7-inch sandwich, grease two sandwich tins and line the base with greaseproof paper. Weigh four eggs and put into a bowl their equal weights in self raising flour, soft margarine and caster sugar.

Break the eggs over these ingredients and add two teaspoons baking powder and 2 tablespoons milk or lemon or orange juice. (If using orange or lemon juice also add the grated rind of the fruit.) With milk add 1 teaspoon vanilla essence.

Beat in a food mixer for 1 minute.

Distribute evenly between the tins and bake in a moderate oven for 15-20 minutes, until the cakes are brown and begin to come away from the sides of the tins.

Turn out onto a wire rack, and when cold sandwich with butter icing or jam. Dredge with icing sugar.

Shortbread

3 lbs plain flour
1 lb block margarine
½ lb butter
12 oz caster sugar

Put all the ingredients into a large mixing bowl and set aside in a warm place to soften. When quite soft knead with the hands until the mixture is moulded together. Press into a tin and bake in a moderate oven until slightly coloured. Dredge with caster sugar and cut into squares. Makes 64 pieces.

Raspberry Fool

Serves 12 to 14

4 lbs fresh or frozen raspberries
1 pint fresh or frozen cream

Thaw berries and cream. Whip cream until thick. Purée the raspberries, and discard the pips.
Mix together and serve chilled with small fingers of shortbread.

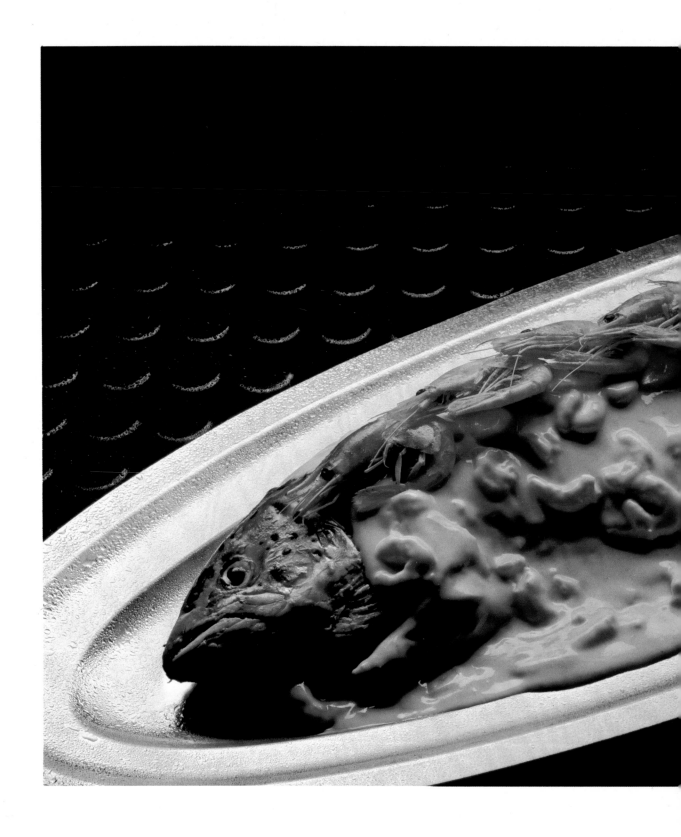

River Add Salmon (Malcolm).

Macnaghten

From Sir Patrick Alexander Macnaghten of Macnaghten, Dundarve, Bushmills, County Antrim, Northern Ireland.

Dundarve is renowned for its steak and kidney pudding which we frequently have for lunch on pheasant shoot days. It does taste better than most other steak and kidney puddings; we believe the rolling of the meat in seasoned flour is important, as is the choice of good fat free steak.

The lemon fluff is so called because it was my wife's recipe and was used here before my father died.

Mrs Patrick's Lemon Fluff

4 level tablespoons caster sugar
4 large eggs, separated
1 top of Jersey milk (not cream which is too heavy)

1 large lemon
½ oz packet powdered gelatine
2 tablespoons boiling water
small macaroons

Beat the sugar and egg yolks together with a wooden spoon, add the top of milk, the lemon juice, the grated rind of half a lemon and finally, the gelatine dissolved in water. Mix well, leave for about 10 minutes until the mixture just begins to solidify (less time if placed in a refrigerator), then fold in the stiffly-beaten egg whites and mix thoroughly. Pour into a serving dish, and put into the refrigerator for at least ½ hour. Just before serving, decorate with the macaroons.

Lettuce Floats

1 cucumber
pineapple pieces
1½ oz shredded almonds
3 tablespoons Hellman's Mayonnaise
   (or a cream dressing)

paprika
4 lettuce leaves

Peel and dice the cucumber, mix with an equal quantity of pineapple pieces and almonds, then add the dressing. Serve individually on a lettuce leaf with a pinch of paprika sprinkled on top.

Dundarve Steak and Kidney Pudding

1 lb flour
1 teaspoon salt
8 oz suet
3 lbs stewing steak

1 ox kidney
seasoned flour
2 large onions
½ pint stock

Mix flour, salt and suet with enough water to enable the mixture to be rolled out. Line a pudding basin with the paste, keeping back enough to form a lid. Cut up the steak and kidney and roll them in the seasoned flour. Finely grate the onions and add them to the steak and kidney, then put the mixture in the basin. Add most of the stock. Cover with suet lid, then greaseproof paper, and steam in a large saucepan for 4 hours. Next day cut a small hole in the suet lid and add a little more stock and steam for 1½ to 2 hours.

Editor: *Here in Scotland I always use spalebone steak for stews and steak and kidney dishes as this meat gives thick gravy, in a natural way.*

Macneil

From Professor Ian R. Macneil of Barra, Kisimul Castle, Barra and Ithaca,
New York

My mother and my Macneil grandmother died when I was quite young and my father was no cook. The result is a hiatus in communication from earlier generations, so that all of our family recipes are those coming from my wife, who comes by her skills through descent as well as inclination.

The Granny Meikle referred to in the recipe was my wife's maternal grandmother who, although she was born in Canada, was a Scot, so perhaps Granny Meikle's Christmas Cake started out as a Scottish recipe.

In spite of the paucity of Macneil of Barra family recipes, the Clan Macneil takes second to none on the culinary front, resting our undisputed laurels on the late, incomparable and delightful F. Marian McNeill.

Lemon Pudding

1 tablespoon butter
1 cup white sugar
2 eggs, separated
2 tablespoons flour
1 cup milk
juice and rind of two lemons

Cream the butter, add the sugar and egg yolks. Add the flour alternately with the milk. Add the lemon juice and rind. Fold in the egg whites, beaten until stiff. Place in a baking dish, and put into a pan of water. Bake at 350° F, 180° C, Gas 4 for about half an hour, until brown on top. The top will be cake-like, the bottom a sauce.

Granny Meikle's Christmas Cake

½ lb butter
1 lb sugar
4 eggs
1 lb flour
½ teaspoon salt
4 teaspoons baking powder
1 cup hot water
1 teaspoon vanilla
1 lb fruit, drained and chopped.

Cream the butter well, add the sugar and then eggs, one at a time. Beat well. Combine the dry ingredients, sift, and add alternately with the hot water. Add the vanilla and finely chopped fruit. Pour into a greased loaf tin (large) or 2 regular size loaf tins. Bake in a cool oven, 300° F, 150° C, Gas 2 for 1½ to 2 hours.

Cooks: *A very good "cutting cake" but less rich than a traditional Christmas Cake.*

Editor: *F. Marian McNeill was the doyen of Scottish cookery writers and is regarded with as much reverence north of the Border as is Mrs Beaton south of the Border.*

Macpherson

From William A. Macpherson of Cluny and Blairgowrie, Newton Castle, Blairgowrie, Perthshire

Here is a recipe from the papers of my great, great, great grandmother, Eliza Dell Macpherson. The original was dated about 1785 but my wife has adapted it and it is now a family favourite.

Pea Soup

approximately 2 oz butter
1½ lb peas
1 cucumber, skinned and chopped
1 small lettuce
½ onion, chopped
mixture of sweet herbs
sprig of mint
salt and pepper

Melt the butter in large saucepan. Add all the ingredients and "sweat" in the butter for about 10 minutes. Add about 1½ pints water, bring to the boil and simmer until tender. Liquidise and reheat before serving.

Opposite: Front left, Susan Catherine's Salmon Mousse (Chisholm); centre front, Lettuce Floats (Macnaghten); right front, Artichaut Froid "Carême" (MacThomas); centre, Avocado Cheese (Leslie); left back, Egg Mousse (Cumming); centre back, Melon Starter (Hamilton).

MacThomas

From Andrew MacThomas of Finegand, Edinburgh

A MacThomas kinsman, one William McCombie of Tillyfour is regarded as the father of the Aberdeen-Angus breed of cattle. No Scottish cookery book should be without this fact so amongst my selection of favourite dishes is an internationally-renowned one using the best of Aberdeen-Angus steak, Beef Wellington.

Beef Wellington

4 lb fillet of beef
freshly ground black pepper
4 oz butter
4 oz button mushrooms
4 oz pâté de foie gras
1½ lb puff pastry
1 egg

Trim any fat from the fillet, roll into a neat shape and tie up at intervals to retain the shape. Melt 2 oz butter in a large frying pan. Fry the meat briskly on all sides to colour. Roast at 425° F, 210° C, Gas 7 for 20 minutes then chill the beef and remove the string.

Slice the mushrooms and sauté them in remaining butter, until soft; leave them to cool then blend with the pâté.

Roll out the prepared pastry to ½ -inch thick, to an oblong 3½ times the width of the fillet, by the length of the fillet plus 7 inches. Spread the pâté over the top of the fillet, place the meat, pâté-side down, in the centre of the pastry. Fold the pastry over and under the meat, brushing the seams carefully with water. Turn the pastry over so that the join is on the underside; prick the top with a fork and decorate with pastry leaves. Cover the pastry and leave in the refrigerator for at least 1 hour.

Beat the egg and brush over the pastry. Put on to a baking tray and bake in the centre of the oven, 425° F, 210° C, Gas 7 for 35 minutes. Place the beef in its pastry on a bed of watercress and serve with broccoli.

Omelette Rothschild

2 egg yolks
3 egg whites
caster sugar
a measure of Grand Marnier
apricot purée·

Beat the eggs, fold together with caster sugar and Grand Marnier, and put into a greased frying pan. Bake in a moderately hot oven for ten minutes. Heat up apricot purée and pour around the edge of the omelette, served on a Number 3 Silver Salver.

Note: *Do not delay in serving this dish, as it will collapse after about 3 minutes.*

Maigrets de Canard Sauvage

Marinate a duck in red wine and diced vegetables, for 24 hours. Fillet the breasts from the duck. Shallow fry in butter according to preference.
  Poach the figs in red wine.
  To make the sauce, reduce the marinade, strain, add the figs and a measure of brandy, and simmer. Pour the sauce over duck, and serve.

Cooks: *The sauce may require thickening. If so, blend two teaspoons of cornflour with water, and add to sauce, stirring all the time, over a medium heat, until the sauce thickens.*

Artichaut Froid "Carême"

Boil one artichoke per person, cool, remove the leaves and centre, leaving the "base" only. Dice a small amount of smoked salmon (Scottish) and envelope in "marie rose" sauce with shrimps. Arrange over artichoke base. Poach an egg and cool. Place on top of arrangement. Cut a slice of Scottish smoked salmon and place over the top. Decorate with a small heart-shaped truffle.

Malcolm

From Robin Malcolm of Poltalloch, Duntrune Castle, Kilmartin, Argyll

---

Duntrune is beside Loch Crinan, into which flows the River Add; we farm part of the Kilmartin Glen. We live off the land, river and sea. Beef and lamb from the farm, vegetables and soft fruit from the garden, salmon and trout from the Add, shellfish and mackerel from the Loch; venison and game if I shoot straight.

We are blessed with the fresh ingredients for any meal, and four healthy children who object to anything "fancy." All our favourite family recipes are therefore very basic. However, surplus produce generally goes to the Cairn Restaurant in Kilmartin, owned by Mr and Mrs Thomson. Her folk have been in this glen as long as mine and what she does with River Add salmon brings customers from far and wide. In the absence of a suitable recipe from our own kitchen, I give you one from Mrs Marion Thomson.

River Add Salmon

3 lbs River Add Salmon

Court Bouillon
¼ pint dry white wine
½ pint water
strip lemon zest

2 bay leaves
1 small carrot
1 small onion
1 clove garlic
1 clove
salt and black peppercorns

Bring the bouillon to the boil, cover and simmer for 10 minutes. Use the fluid to poach the salmon in. When the salmon is cooked, the meat loosens from the bone.

Carefully remove salmon from the Court Bouillon which should now be strained and retained. Skin and fillet the fish before dividing it into eight pieces.

Sauce
3 oz butter
3 oz flour

1 pint single cream
8 oz cooked and shelled Loch Crinan
    prawns (frozen prawns may be used)

In a deep pan melt the butter, add the flour and make a roux. Cook for a few moments, but do not brown, then add the Court Bouillon. Bring the sauce mixture to the boil, stirring continuously and allow to simmer and cook. After a few minutes slowly pour in the cream and gently fold in the prawns; then adjust seasoning.

To serve
Lift the salmon carefully onto a heated plate, pour the sauce over, and garnish with twists of lemon and sprigs of parsley.

Matheson

From Major Sir Torquhil Matheson of Matheson, Frome, Somerset

In the mid-16th century Macdonald of Glengarry wished to pick a quarrel with Dugald Roy Matheson, with whom he shared the Lochalsh rents.

He was aware that MacMathon was notoriously prejudiced against goat flesh and that it would be a studied insult to present it to him. He therefore ordered a lamb to be fed on goat's milk and invited the other to dine with him at a castle he possessed (the ruins of which can be seen at Loch Acha-na-hinich today). Matheson was so unsuspecting that he attended the castle, accompanied only by his Gillie Mor (his Champion) instead of his usual retinue of twelve.

The first dish set on the table was the lamb, fed on goat's milk. On tasting it, he rejected it, imagining it to be kid. His host asked what objection he had to the dish and he angrily replied "You know I do not eat goat's flesh." Glengarry asserted that Matheson had never eaten of more genuine mutton but Matheson pertinaciously insisted upon it being goat.

From this dispute arose the quarrel Glengarry had expected; Dugald Roy was immediately overpowered, bound and conveyed prisoner to Invergarry where he died in confinement "from the effect of this indignity."

This family tale comes from the Bennetsfield M.S. and is reproduced in the History of the Mathesons by Mackenzie and MacBain, published in 1900.

Potato Soup

Serves 5 or 6

3 oz dripping
2 large onions
2 lbs potatoes (peeled and sliced)
3 pints water

salt and pepper
chopped parsley
2½ oz oatmeal

Melt fat and fry onions for a few minutes. Add potatoes, water and seasonings. Boil gently for ½ hour. Sprinkle in oatmeal slowly and boil for another 10 minutes. Sprinkle chopped parsley just before serving.

Venison Pie (cold)

2 lbs venison (raw)
1 lb deer's liver*
chopped onions
pepper and salt
hot bacon fat

thin slices of bacon
chopped parsley
cooked deer's tongue
good venison stock
glass of port

Mince the venison (no fat or sinew) and liver. Add a teaspoon of onion, salt and pepper. Mix very well and fry lightly in hot bacon fat. Cover the bottom of a pie dish with thin slices of bacon. Put in a thin layer of the fry. Sprinkle with chopped parsley and coarse ground pepper. Add a layer of thin slices of deer's tongue. Then start again with a layer of bacon—then fry—then flavouring and tongue, etc., until a pie dish is full. Add a breakfast cup of good venison stock and a wine glass (claret size) of port. Stand the pie dish in a tin of water and put in a moderate oven, tightly covered with foil. Cook for 2½-3 hours, watching the water—and topping up with stock if necessary. (Improved by layers of *raw* grouse, hare or duck.)

*Do not use stag's liver late in the season.

Marmalade

Makes about 20 lbs

6 Seville oranges
1 lemon
4 pints water
4 lbs sugar

Wash the oranges and lemon and boil in water for about 20 minutes. Take out one at a time and cut into 8 or 10 segments and return, keeping the water boiling. Boil for a further 20 minutes or more. Add the sugar gradually, stirring enough to keep it from sticking. As the pips rise to the top, skim them off until they are all well away. Test for setting and pour into 7-lb stone jars when ready. Seal at once (use cling film and foil).
  Note: This makes an excellent quick pudding liquidized with vanilla ice cream and partly re-frozen for about ½ hour—about ¼ marmalade to ¾ ice cream.

Plum Chutney

3 lbs slightly unripe plums
1 lb green apples
1 lb onions
1 teaspoon mixed spice
1 teaspoon ginger
1 teaspoon cinnamon

$\frac{1}{4}$ teaspoon cayenne pepper
$\frac{1}{2}$ lb sugar (dark brown 'pieces')
1 lb sultanas
$\frac{3}{4}$ pint cider (or other) vinegar
$\frac{3}{4}$ pint water (replace with malt vinegar
  if required)

Stone and slice plums. Peel and slice apples and onions. Boil whole lot together for $\frac{1}{2}$ hour.

Editor: *You will see the Mathesons do not include a recipe using goat flesh nor even one using mutton —just in case!*

Menzies

From The Menzies of Menzies, Dalkeith, Western Australia

From November to April, prawns are plentiful in the Swan river which flows through Perth, Western Australia. On a hot summer night, it is fun to trawl for them with a net and then have my wife cook them in her own special way.

Whisky Prawns

1 lb prawns (shells on)
4 tablespoons butter
4 tablespoons olive oil
2 tablespoons chopped shallots
1 clove garlic
2 peeled tomatoes
salt and pepper
cayenne pepper

6 tablespoons whisky
6 tablespoons dry white wine
1 teaspoon cornflour
4 tablespoons cream
1 egg yolk
pinch tarragon
boiled rice

Combine butter and oil in pan. Add shallots and garlic and fry gently. Now add shelled prawns, tomatoes, salt, pepper, and cayenne pepper to taste. Fry for a few more minutes. Pour over 4 tablespoons of whisky and flame. Add dry white wine and simmer gently for 5 minutes. Remove prawns and keep them warm in the oven. Mix the rest of the whisky with the cornflour, cream, egg yolk and tarragon. Add this mixture to the pan and beat hard over a high flame until the sauce boils and thickens. Return prawns to pan and mix in with the sauce. Serve on a bed of boiled rice.

Cooks: *The Scots often see it as sacrilege to add good Scotch to food, but in this case the fine flavour achieved makes the addition well worth while.*

Opposite: Clockwise from window: Speybank Favourite Fruit Mousse with Glayva (Glayva); Turkey Cranberry Salad Ecosse (Glayva); Vintage Liqueur Marmalade Flan (Glayva); Caledonian Cream (Borthwick).

Moncreiffe

From Sir Iain Moncreiffe of that Ilk, (Albany Herald), Easter Moncreiffe, Perth

My great-aunt Georgina Moncreiffe, Countess of Dudley, was one of the most celebrated of Victorian beauties. Indeed, the Shah of Persia, on seeing her at a Court Ball, said he would like to buy her: to which the reply was that her husband could afford to buy Persia. In a way this was true, in those days before the discovery of oil, as Lord Dudley had an income of a thousand golden sovereigns a day. But Aunt Georgie also compiled *The Dudley Book of Cookery and Household Recipes.* Perhaps my favourite recipe in her book is "Devilled Quails." But in my own case, it is important to leave out the "eschalot" (shallot) as—like some other Moncreiffes—I was born with an allergy to the whole garlic and onion clan.

For an "every-day" recipe, one of my favourites is Fish Pie.

Devilled Quails

Bone the quails as you would for a galantine of chicken; beat them lightly to flatten, then sauté them on one side of their skin for two minutes, then turn and sauté them again for one minute. The quails by this means are almost cooked, and grilling finishes the cooking. To devil them use melted butter with English mustard and Worcester sauce, and serve them with a sauce brune mixed with vinegar, eschalot, Harvey, Worcester. Pass through a muslin and serve separately.

Cooks: *A delicious dish, but two or three quails are required to satisfy a man-size appetite. See recipe for sauce diable on page 111.*

Fish Pie

1 lb fish   seasoning
2 oz butter   2 hard boiled eggs
½-¾ pint milk   1 lb mashed potatoes
1 oz flour

Cook the fish in milk, strain it, retaining milk. Flake the fish, and make a white sauce with the milk, butter and flour. Add a little cream if desired, and season. Put in a buttered casserole dish and top with hard-boiled eggs. Cover with creamy mashed potatoes. Lightly brown under the grill.

Editor: *Like Scotland's Clan Chiefs, quails are birds of passage and have been described as "the aristocracy of the bird world."*

The birds can be found in Europe during the spring and summer months but they return to warmer climes before winter comes in. When plucked and presented, they are a little smaller than a pigeon.

Morrison

From Iain M. Morrison of Ruchdi, Isle of North Uist, Western Isles

---

Our family favourites are simple but good and include Granny's Scotch Broth. Although my wife has made Granny's Scotch Broth many times, I'm afraid like so many husbands, I tell her it's not as good as Granny's!

Marinade for Barbecue Lamb Chops

1 level teaspoon English Vineyard
   Mustard
ground black pepper
2 tablespoons red wine

1 tablespoon lemon juice
1 finely chopped onion
½ teaspoon mixed herbs
1 crushed clove of garlic

Combine the above ingredients and leave the chops to marinade for as long as possible. This is also marvellous for sausages.

Cooks: *The marinade will not only impart flavour to the meat, but the acid in a marinade (which may be wine, vinegar, lemon juice or tomato juice) acts as a meat tenderiser. Marinade meat the day before cooking, if possible.*

Flapjacks

6 oz butter
4 oz brown sugar
8 oz rolled Scottish oats
pinch ginger

Melt the fat and add sugar and oats and mix well. Turn into a flat baking tray and press down evenly and then cook for 15-20 minutes at 350°F, 180°C, Gas 4.

Granny's Scotch Broth

1 neck of lamb or lamb stock
2 onions, finely sliced
3 carrots, grated
4 leeks
½ small turnip, grated
garlic
salt and black pepper
1 cup pearl barley, soaked overnight
1 cup dried peas, soaked overnight (these
    must be the large variety and are known
    in our family as bullet peas)

Granny cooks everything together in one large stock pot and adds the final touch just before serving—as much chopped parsley as can be found.

Editor: *My mother makes her broth this way–no sweating of vegetables. Everything goes in at one time and it too is delicious. But I never make it as well as she does, she tells me!*

Murray of Atholl

From The Duke of Atholl, Blair Castle, Blair Atholl

This is not technically a recipe, but it used to be very popular and is unique to the Atholls. Personally I think it is rather a waste of good whisky.

Atholl Brose

Over 200 years ago, when the Highlander was trekking across country and never knew when or where he might eat, he took with him a bag of oatmeal and some spirit, usually home brew. This provided him with enough sustenance until he was able to reach normal food once again.

However, in the 19th century, there was a tremendous vogue for resurrecting old customs (just as there is today) and this was done with the oatmeal and whisky; honey was added to the mixture, to make it palatable, and gradually Atholl Brose developed into the drink we know today.

1st Version

To Make one quart
Take 4 dessertspoons of run honey, 4 sherry glasses of prepared oatmeal. Stir these well together and put into a quart bottle; fill up with whisky. Shake well before serving.
To prepare the oatmeal
Put a handful of oatmeal into a basin and mix with cold water to the consistency of a paste (thick).

Pass the oatmeal through a fine strainer, taking care not to make the oatmeal too watery.

2nd Version

Strain a handful of oatmeal through a fine sieve into a basin and mix with cold water to the consistency of a thick paste. Be careful not to make it too watery. Add four dessertspoons of run honey to four sherry glasses of the sieved oatmeal. Stir well together and put into a quart bottle. Fill up with whisky. Shake well before serving. Can be drunk at once or kept indefinitely if well corked and sealed. The bottle should be kept standing upright.

Some ladies like a little cream added to it.

3rd Version

½ pint oatmeal
1 dessertspoon honey
½ pint whisky
1 tablespoon cream

The oatmeal should be soaked overnight and then put through a fine strainer. Mix honey and whisky together in a basin and when properly mixed add the strained oatmeal and cream. Cream is not recommended if "The Brose" is to be kept any length of time, as it is inclined to get sour and is only added to give a little colour. "The Brose" should be well shaken before drinking. It is sometimes necessary to add a little more whisky if "The Brose" has been left for a day or two, as the meal absorbs the whisky. The rawer the whisky the better for "Atholl Brose" with mild whisky does not result in a full flavour.

This is a drink that fills and satisfies.

Editor: *I had the pleasure of meeting the Atholl Highlanders, whilst writing this book. The only private army in Europe, they tell me they were weaned on Atholl Brose–but behind the beards I detected a grin and there was a twinkle in the eye as it was said.*

Ogilvy

From The Earl of Airlie, Cortachy Castle, Kirriemuir, Angus

Salmon Plait

½ lb puff pastry
½ pint thick white sauce
8 oz left-over salmon or sea trout
7 oz tin sweetcorn
fresh parsley
2 hard boiled eggs

Roll out the puff pastry quite thinly. Make a white sauce and flake salmon into sauce. Add corn and plenty of chopped parsley. Spread this on the thinly-rolled pastry and place sliced eggs on the top. Plait the pastry over the top. Brush with egg and milk. Bake at 375°F, 190°C, Gas 5 for ½ hour.

Cooks: *Tinned red salmon could be substituted for the left-over salmon.*

Cold Spinach Soufflé

½ pint whipping cream
1 lb cooked spinach
1 tin Campbell's consommé
1 envelope gelatine
salt and pepper

Whip the cream and fold into the puréed spinach. Add the consommé and dissolved gelatine. Add salt and pepper and pour into a mould or soufflé dish. Garnish the top with crushed crisp bacon.

Cooks: *See notes on gelatine on page 52.*

Devilled Grouse

Serves 6

3 grouse
3 oz patna rice
1 tin Campbell's consommé
1 bay leaf
curry powder
2 oz sultanas
½ pint cream

2 tablespoons Worcester sauce
1 teaspoon Bovril
2 tablespoons sauce diable (see below)

Dress grouse as for roasting and place in oven covered by good dripping and tinfoil. Leave for 30 minutes in a hot oven (375°F, 190°C, Gas 5). Put rice in small pan and cover with consommé. Add the bay leaf plus one teaspoon curry powder and sultanas. Allow to simmer very slowly until rice is cooked and nearly dry. Avoid stirring. Remove grouse from oven and cut each bird cleanly in half. Place in a serving dish and allow to cool, then cover with whipped cream mixed with Worcester sauce, Bovril and sauce diable. Place cooked rice round about bird halves and put back in hot oven for 10 minutes to heat through and serve at once with the usual vegetables.

Sauce Diable

1 tablespoon olive oil
2 finely chopped onions
1 crushed clove garlic
1 level tablespoon flour
1 level tablespoon Dijon mustard
1 tablespoon white wine vinegar
⅓ pint beef stock
2 level teaspoons soft brown sugar
¼ teaspoon Worcester sauce

1 teaspoon chopped capers
1 bay leaf
salt and pepper

Heat oil and fry onions and garlic until golden brown. Stir in flour. Add mustard and vinegar and gradually stir in the stock. Bring sauce to the boil, stirring all the time. When thick add sugar, Worcester sauce, capers and bay leaf and season with salt and pepper.
Simmer for 5-10 minutes stirring frequently.

Ramsay

From the Earl of Dalhousie, Brechin Castle, Brechin, Angus

Marinated Venison Steaks

4 thick steaks of venison cut from
  the loin
salt and freshly ground black pepper
½ Spanish onion, sliced
2 carrots, sliced
4 sprigs parsley
2 bay leaves
thyme and rosemary
¼ pint dry white wine
olive oil
2 tablespoons butter

Sauce
2 tablespoons butter
2 shallots, finely chopped
1 tablespoon flour
6 tablespoons marinade juices,
  strained
⅓ pint sour cream
lemon juice
freshly ground black pepper

Season venison steaks generously with salt and freshly ground black pepper, and mix in a bowl with sliced onion and carrots, parsley, bay leaves, thyme and rosemary. Moisten with dry white wine and 6 tablespoons olive oil. Place bowl in the fridge and marinate steaks for 24 to 48 hours, turning them occasionally.

To cook steaks:
Remove venison from marinade, reserving marinade juices for further use, and pat dry. Heat 2 tablespoons each olive oil and butter in a large thick-bottomed frying pan, and sauté venison over a high heat for about 3 minutes on each side. Remove and keep warm. Serve steaks on a heated serving dish with sauce.

Sauce:
Drain excess fat from frying pan and add 2 tablespoons butter. Sauté finely chopped shallots until soft; sprinkle with flour and cook, stirring until the roux is lightly browned. Add 6 tablespoons strained marinade juices, the sour cream and lemon juice, and freshly ground black pepper to taste.

112

Rattray

From Captain James Rattray of Rattray, Ranelagh, Dublin

The family home, at Craighall-Rattray in Perthshire, is where Joe Beech, formerly of the Coldstream Guards, used to cook for the family. Craighall Chicken was one of his specialities.

Chicken Craighall

1 roasting chicken
1 apple
butter
4 rashers back bacon
cloves and powdered cloves
salt and pepper

Sauce
1 oz butter
1 oz flour
milk as required
2 hard boiled eggs
chopped parsley

Stuff the chicken with the apple and rub it with butter. Lay bacon across the breast and skewer with the cloves. Sprinkle clove powder on the bacon to taste. Rub the legs generously with butter and roast in a moderate oven (350°F, 180°C, Gas 4) until chicken and bacon are cooked. Pierce the side of the chicken to see if the juices are clear. Meanwhile, for the sauce make a béchamel with flour and milk, add the chopped egg and season as required. Serve egg sauce in a sauceboat with chopped parsley.

Rhubarb Pudding

Take young rhubarb, chop and simmer with minimum water and heather honey. Serve cold and strain. Serve double cream in a separate sauce boat.

Robertson (Donnachaidh)

From Langton Robertson of Struan, Jamaica, British West Indies

After my son Gilbert married, I have many very happy memories of visiting him and his wife Bridget at their home in England. I remember with pleasure the Chicken Paprika which Bridget served for my first meal in Britain and I pass this on as one of my favourite dishes.

Living, as I do, in Jamaica, my favourite sweet is one which is readily available here but which can easily be made in most other parts of the world where coconuts are on sale. I thoroughly recommend its use with almost any pudding.

Chicken Paprika

Serves 6

1 chicken joint per person
1 onion, chopped
1 gill wine or vermouth
2 gills stock
½ lb tomatoes
1 green pepper
½ lb mushrooms
1 dessertspoon paprika
2 oz shelled walnuts

Roll the chicken in seasoned flour and fry until brown. Add chopped onion and fry for one minute. Put all the ingredients, except walnuts, into a casserole and simmer for 20 minutes, either on top of the cooker or in the oven. Add the walnuts and cook for another 30 minutes.

Coconut Cream

Mainly served with fruit salad, but can be used on almost any other pudding.

Remove the flesh from a coconut and peel off the brown backing. Grate the flesh into a bowl and cover with boiling water. When cold, press this mixture through a sieve, squeezing the coconut as hard as possible to remove the liquid. Leave the liquid in the refrigerator for an hour or two. The top layer of the liquid will become really thick and can be used separately from the rest if liked, or the two parts may be mixed together.

Editor: *Langton Robertson of Struan was born in Jamaica and has lived there all his life. He became Chief of the clan in 1949 on the death of his father. Now retired, he was historian at Munro College, Jamaica.*

Rollo

From Lord Rollo, Pitcairns, Dunning, Perthshire

Gaspacho

1½ lbs tomatoes, ripe
1 very small onion, chopped fine
   (about 2 teaspoons)
1 clove of garlic, crushed
½ green pepper
¼ pint chicken stock

2 slices brown bread (no crust)
salt and pepper
2 tablespoons olive oil or
   sunflower seed oil
1 tablespoon cider vinegar

Skin and seed the tomatoes, take seeds out of pepper and slice. Put all the ingredients in a blender, except the oil and vinegar; blend, then add oil and vinegar and the salt and pepper. Serve ice-cold with cucumber cut in small squares and croûtons of fried bread (cold).

Steak au Poivre

Use 1 fillet steak per person, about 1¼ inches thick and fairly large. Crush about 2 tablespoons black peppercorns. Trim the fillets and press into the peppercorns. Fry in a little oil for 6 minutes, turning occasionally. Serve with lots of garlic or parsley butter on top, and fried mushrooms.

Syllabub

¼ pint sweet sherry
2 tablespoons brandy (cooking)
1 tablespoon caster sugar

juice of 1 lemon
½ pint cream

Whip all together. To go with strawberries or fruit salad.

Cure for Deafness

Roast an onion before bedtime. Put an inner division of it into the ear affected, as warm as the patient can bear it. Keep it in with a warm flannel bandage till morning, in the course of which perspiration will be excited and on being taken away the impediment will be removed and the hearing restored, if the directions here given are carefully attended to.

Sour Crout

(Take 20 common cabbages . . .)

Chop them well then put a little salt at the bottom of tub, then a layer of the chopped cabbage, about an inch thick. Press it with a wooden pestle till the juice appears then put in the same quantity of salt and cabbage as at first and so on till you fill the tub. Every layer must be pressed. When done set the tub in a warm place to ferment and when it is fermented and smells sour you must put it in a cool place with a weight on the top of the cabbage to keep the juice above the cabbage else it will spoil. In ten days it will be fit for use.

Ginger Beer

Take 1½ oz of ginger—well bruised, 1 oz Cream of Tartar, and 1 lb of white sugar. Put these ingredients into an earthen vessel and pour upon them a gallon of boiling water. When cold add a tablespoonful of yeast and let the whole stand till next morning, then skim it, bottle it and keep it 3 days in a cool place before you drink it. Be sure to use good corks and secure them with twine or wire.

Recipe from Lady Rollo circa 1887.

Editor: *Lord Rollo's personal selection of "favourite dishes" is a very international one but it has been augmented by a selection which I have made from his collection of old family recipe books, hand written, and dating from around 1880. The Hon Mrs Carstairs Bruce of Tillycoultry, whose name appears on one of these books, must have had a great love of ginger beer and ginger wine as several recipes for each have been meticulously noted. The one I give here is from Lady Rollo, dated 1887. Ginger, of course, together with many other spices from the Orient and India, was very popular around that time.*

I have also included a highly original cure for deafness because of its culinary content. It's not difficult to imagine how it works.

Rose

From Miss Elizabeth Rose, Baroness of Kilravock, Kilravock Castle, Inverness

---

Our cook, Mrs Nicholson, produces a very fine curry and shortbread which, although made with margarine, has a very buttery flavour.

Rose Clan Shortbread

½ lb margarine (butter will not do)   12 oz plain flour
2 oz caster sugar   ½ teaspoon salt

Mix all the ingredients in mixer bowl. Blend together until pliable. Knead and roll out to about ¼-inch thick. Cut into shapes. Bake in a warm oven, 325°F, 160°C, Gas 3 for 25 minutes until pale golden brown. Take out of oven and immediately sprinkle with caster sugar.

Cooks: *Extremely light and short in texture.*

Mrs Nicholson's Curry

1 lb stewing beef or minced beef   1 tin of Le Karnie Curry Paste
oil for cooking   (or other brand)
2 onions (finely chopped)   1 tablespoon cornflour
2 green apples (chopped)   1 tablespoon Bisto
2 handfuls raisins   2 tablespoons of Vencat Curry Powder
½ pint beef stock   (or more if desired)
pepper and salt to taste

Brown the meat in the oil. Add the onions, apples, raisins and the beef stock. Simmer for 1½ hours. Add the rest of ingredients and cook for another ½ hour.
   Serve with boiled rice.
   Side dishes: Poppadoms, fried onions, grilled bacon (chopped), coconut, bananas (sliced), Mango Chutney, sliced tomato, sliced pineapple, chopped hard-boiled eggs.

Mrs
with

1 loin of
8 oz can
½ pint w
2 oz blac
1 level te
¼ level t

Place th
Blend t
over the
Gas 4-5
cooked
redcurr
cooker
Serve
Note

Cooks
adjust

Dr

Wher
ready
or all
the T
betw
Carr
of th

Coo

Edit
Ente
sout

A selection of baking photographed in the Georgian Kitchen, Charlotte Square, Edinburgh, courtesy of the National Trust for Scotland.

Shaw

From John Shaw of Tordarroch, Farr, Inverness

During the turbulent Jacobite times some 200 years ago in the Highlands, the brave itinerant Episcopalian Bishop Forbes described in his Journal his visit to the Shaws of Tordarroch in June 1770:

"At Tordarroch, Ellrig and Letterwhealin, we were so elegantly and even sumptuously entertained; eight, nine or ten dishes on the table with deserts." He went on to describe the abundance of beef and veal, mutton and lamb, goat flesh, trout, salmon and roe, geese, turkeys, ducks and poultry. His host told him "every dish we put on the table we have in our own farms, only we must give out a little money for wine, tea and sugar."

Little of the tradition of cooking has been handed down to us, but my wife gives a few recipes which we often use, some Scottish and some from our journeys overseas, which might be of interest to those who follow this generation.

Porridge

scant 3 pints cold water
1 level teaspoon sea salt

1 slightly heaped teacup of fine or medium oatmeal (not flaked oats)

Pour the water into a pan and sprinkle the oatmeal over the surface of the water. Add the salt. Bring slowly to the boil, stirring all the time and then gently simmer for about 30 minutes, stirring from time to time.

To save time, porridge can be prepared the previous night, simmering for ten minutes only. Put a lid on the pot and leave to stand until morning, when you should stir gently and possibly add a little boiling water.

Serve with cream poured over each helping.

Porridge is not supposed to be eaten with sugar, although children and a few others have non-Highland tastes and prefer to add a little when it has been served. In the old days, it was eaten from a silver "porringer," a small bowl with a single handle, sometimes made in the shape of a leaf. Traditionally each person was given a cup of cream and they dipped each spoonful of porridge into the cream which avoided cooling the porridge by pouring the cream over it.

It is said that it was the custom to stroll around the room after each mouthful, to aid digestion!

Fish Soup

I developed the idea for this recipe from Majorcan households where various kinds of fish are used for making soup.

Clean the fish thoroughly, but leave the heads on, as these add to the flavour. Put the fish in a large pan with three or four pints of water according to the quantity of fish (the stock needs to be quite well flavoured, so the volume of water must not "swamp" it). Add three medium-sized chopped onions, a clove of garlic, four peeled tomatoes, a bay leaf and a little fennel if you have it. Bring to the boil and simmer for about one hour.

When cooked, put the stock through a sieve and shred any good pieces of fish, adding them to the stock. Season and bring back to the boil, adding half a teacup of rice to every pint of stock. Simmer with the lid on until the rice is cooked, then add a good quantity of chopped parsley.

Note: In our part of the world, perch is plentiful in the lochs, probably the descendents of the fish originally brought here by the monks. As they are rather bony and full of scales when fried, I find them excellent for this kind of soup.

Tortilla con Patatas

We spent some time in Majorca and were often invited to homes there. I was given this very adaptable recipe for potato omelette which is cooked in much the same way as a Spanish omelette. It can be served hot or cold and can even be used as a sandwich filling on a picnic.

1 medium size potato per person
olive oil or cooking oil
2 eggs per person

salt, pepper
chopped parsley

Peel potatoes and cut into small pieces as for making "chipped" potatoes. Fry in a heavy pan in a little oil until cooked and slightly brown. Put aside and keep warm.

Beat the eggs and season, adding chopped parsley. Do not add milk.

Heat a dessertspoonful of oil in the omelette pan until it is quite hot. Pour in the egg mixture to a depth of ½-¾ inch. Quickly add some of the potatoes and stir them in.

Cook the omelette until it is firm underneath but still moist on top, as it has to be turned completely over.

To do this, loosen the omelette all round with a fish slice. Place a plate on top of the pan then invert pan and plate. Hopefully the omelette will be lying face down on the plate! Add a little more oil to the pan, heat it then slide the omelette back into the pan, uncooked side down. Cook for a further minute or so then slide off on to a serving dish.

This omelette should not be kept hot as it begins to taste sulphurous. It should either be served at once or just left to cool naturally. It is also a delicious dish with boiled broad beans instead of potatoes.

Roast Beef

4 lbs topside of beef (or "salmon cut")
  well hung
rosemary, thyme and bay leaves
  (dried, if you have none fresh)
sea salt and black pepper
olive oil

Place the meat in a roasting tin and sprinkle lightly with fine sea salt and freshly ground black pepper. Scatter with rosemary leaves, thyme and six bay leaves. Pour a little olive (or sunflower) oil over the joint then add half a teacup of water to the bottom of the roasting tin. Cover the meat with foil.

Roast at 400°-425°F, 200°-210°C, Gas 6-7. After 15 minutes, baste the meat; check it from time to time. The water in the tin should have diminished and a brown sediment have begun to form. Before this begins to burn add a little more water as the basis of a good-coloured gravy. When necessary, add a little more water.

Cooking time should be about 1-1¼ hours if the meat is to be brown on the outside and still pink inside.

Ten minutes before it is cooked, take the foil off and pour a glass of sherry over the meat. It should then be returned to the oven, uncovered, to brown a little.

Place the meat on an "ashet,"—the Scots word for an oval meat plate—and keep it warm.

To make the gravy: allow the sediment from the meat to cool a little. Stir in a heaped dessertspoon of plain flour and gradually add ½-1 pint of water from the vegetable cooking (keep vegetable water for sauces and soups!). Slowly bring to the boil, stirring all the time. The gravy should not be too thick. Cook it for a few minutes, strain, season and keep hot until required.

Note: In ancient Greece, according to Homer's Odyssey, the meat was rolled in oatmeal before cooking. This Scottish-sounding method is excellent but of course you should omit the rosemary and other herbs.

Editor: *It would be unthinkable to have a* Clans Cook Book *without a recipe for porridge, and Mrs Shaw of Tordarroch gives two versions. For centuries, oatmeal has been part of the staple diet of the Highlands. Dr Samuel Johnson described oats as "a grain which in England is generally given to horses, but in Scotland supports the people."*

Stirling

From Sir Charles Stirling, Farnham, Surrey

Chestnut Soup

Serves 4

1 oz butter
½ lb chestnuts
1 onion
2 oz celery
1 small carrot
½ pint each of stock and creamy milk
¼ teaspoon each of salt and sugar
1 sprig of thyme
1 stalk of parsley

Melt the butter in a heavy pan. Add the shelled chestnuts and thinly sliced vegetables and let them brown very slightly before adding the heated stock, seasoning and herbs. Simmer gently for ½ hour and pass the contents of the pan through an electric blender (removing the thyme first). Just before serving add the cream or milk and reheat. The soup should not boil.

Cooks: *Dried chestnuts may also be used. Soak in water overnight then drain and use as fresh chestnuts.*

Editor: *I first tried Chestnut Soup at Houston House Hotel, near Edinburgh where it was on their "no choice" menu. Made with chicken stock, it was delicious and is now on my personal list of dinner party dishes.*

Sutherland

From the Countess of Sutherland, House of Tongue, Lairg, Sutherland

We are lucky enough to live by the sea with a sheltered walled garden. As we have loch and kyle fishing, we eat a lot of sea fish, trout (brown and sea trout), home-grown vegetables and salad. We also have excellent mussels and cockles on our doorstep, so to speak, as well as lobsters and scampi.

Mackerel Pâté

3 medium mackerel, gutted
2-3 oz butter
2-3 fl oz double cream,
    or 2-3 tablespoons crowdie

7 teaspoons lemon juice
salt and freshly ground black pepper
Tabasco

Poach the fish in water and a squeeze of lemon juice, bouquet garni and black peppercorns. Cool in liquid. Skin and bone fish and pound until smooth (or put in blender). Work in butter which has been well creamed. Add seasonings and then cream. Turn into mould and chill for several hours. Serve with toast or hot brown bread.

Smoked Trout or Smoked Mackerel Pâté

1 smoked trout or smoked mackerel
juice of one lemon
4 oz fresh unsalted cream cheese

freshly ground black pepper
½ teaspoon paprika
salt (optional)

Skin and fillet fish. Put through a blender with the lemon juice. Work in cream cheese thoroughly. Season with pepper and paprika, and possibly salt and more lemon juice. Press into a terrine and cool for several hours. Serve with hot toast.

126

Roast Leg of Lamb

Take off the excess fat. Make about 10 incisions in leg and insert a few rosemary leaves. Sprinkle with black pepper. Cook on a rack in a baking tin. Seal in a hot oven, 450° F, 230°C, Gas 8 for 15 minutes. Pour over a wine glass of red wine and ⅔ of a glass of home made stock with a sprig of rosemary in it. Baste well and cook at 375° F, 150°C, Gas 5, allowing 20 minutes per pound.
  Serve with mint jelly.

Pear Water Ice

½ lb granulated sugar
¾ pint water
2 lbs pears
2 lemons

Melt the sugar in water. Peel the pears. Poach the cores and peel for a few minutes. Strain and then poach the pears gently in the syrup until soft. Remove, bring the syrup to the boil for one minute, and then cool. Put the pears through a blender and add to the syrup with the lemon juice. Freeze for at least 4 hours. Serve with a twist of lemon peel.

Crab Apple and Mint Jelly

4 lbs crab apples
6 cloves
1 inch stem ginger
rind and juice of one lemon
water to cover

1 lb sugar to each pint strained liquid
1 large bunch of mint
¾ gill white wine vinegar
green colouring if wished

Halve the crab apples and remove any blemished parts. Place in a pan with cloves, ginger, lemon rind and juice, and cover with water. Cover, bring to the boil and simmer gently until tender and pulpy. Ladle into a scalded jelly bag which has been suspended over a suitable container; leave to drip for several hours. Do not squeeze the cloth because this would cause the jelly to be cloudy. Measure the strained liquid back into a pan, add warmed sugar, dissolve gently and then bring to the boil. After a few minutes add the mint stalks which have been tied together, and the vinegar. Boil until a good set is obtained. Add the finely chopped mint, colour, if liked, and bottle. Store in a cool dry place.

Urquhart

From Kenneth Trist Urquhart of Urquhart, Jefferson, Louisiana, U.S.A.

At the party given in honour of the Two Hundredth Anniversary of the establishment of the Urquhart Family in New Orleans, which was held in conjunction with the Fourth Annual General Meeting of the worldwide Clan Urquhart Association, in December 1979, Bourbon Sweet Potatoes and Minty Carrots, part of the buffet dinner of Scottish and Creole dishes, were great favourites of the large number of guests who attended and proclaimed them ideal complements to the Artillery Punch and Atholl Brose, which were the drinks of the evening.

Artillery Punch is a favourite drink at Urquhart Clan gatherings. It is a traditional drink of the Old South in the United States, having originally been served at military balls of the Earl of Chatham's Artillery in Savannah, Georgia during colonial days. I was introduced to it when I was an officer of the famed Washington Artillery of New Orleans, and it has been a favourite of mine ever since. I have varied the traditional recipe slightly, in order to give it a Scottish touch reminiscent of the Jacobite heritage of Clan Urquhart, by substituting Drambuie for Benedictine. For this reason, my version is often referred to as "Urquhart's Artillery Punch."

Artillery Punch

1 quart champagne
3 quarts plain cold tea
2 cups sugar
1 quart mixed lime, lemon and
   orange juice
1 quart brandy
1 quart bourbon whisky

1 quart sweet wine
1 quart rum
½ pint Drambuie
1 pint gin
pineapple chunks
cherries

Mix tea and juices together. Add sugar and stir until dissolved. Add liquors. Let stand for 24 hours, then place a lump of ice in a punch bowl and pour the mixture over it. Add one quart of chilled champagne to each bowl of mixture before serving.

Cooks: *We are sure we loved it, but have somehow forgotten. The only advice we can give is not culinary–just order a taxi!*

Flat Rock Pudding

For generations, Plum Pudding has been an important holiday dessert of the Urquharts, especially for their traditional Christmas dinner. During the American Civil War, the family, staunchly loyal to the Confederacy, refused to live in New Orleans during its occupation by the Union forces. They retired to their country estate at Flat Rock in the mountains of western North Carolina. Scarcity of many things in the mountains required the Urquharts to improvise frequently.

During their first Christmas at Flat Rock, Mrs Robert Dow Urquhart, my great grandmother, found herself without the customary raisins and currants for the family's Plum Pudding. She substituted dried whortleberries in their place and found that the pudding she produced was very nice. Thus was born Flat Rock Pudding, made with blueberries instead of raisins and currants. Since the War the pudding, first produced at Flat Rock in December 1862, has taken its place with the traditional plum pudding as a popular holiday dessert in my home.

¾ lb beef suet, or ½ cup shortening
¾ lb (or 4 cups) breadcrumbs
½ lb (or 1 cup) flour
2 lbs blueberries*
1 cup chopped walnuts (optional)
½ lb citron (or lemon) and orange peel
½ teaspoon nutmeg

⅛ teaspoon ginger
9 eggs
½ teaspoon salt
½ teaspoon baking powder
1 cup sugar
1 wineglass brandy

Chop the suet as fine as possible and mix it (or the shortening) with the breadcrumbs and flour; add the blueberries, walnuts, citron and orange peel cut in thin slices and mix all together with the nutmeg and ginger; then stir in the 9 eggs well beaten, the salt, the baking powder, the sugar, and the brandy; and again mix so that all the ingredients are moistened. Pour into a well-greased 1½ to 2 quart mold. Cover tightly with a glass lid or aluminium foil. Place the mold in a pot of gently bubbling hot water.

The water should come half way up the sides of the mold; and should be refilled during steaming, being careful not to get any water into mold mixture. Throughout steaming maintain water at a gentle boil, with burner set on medium. Keep the pot covered and steam pudding for about 2-2½ hours. Remove mold from water; and let stand for five minutes before unmolding. Pudding should be served on a plate garnished with holly leaves and berries. The top of the pudding may also be garnished in this manner; or the pudding may be covered with a brandy sauce.

*For variety, 3 cups of whole berry cranberry sauce (either homemade or canned) may be substituted.

Virginia Mint Julep

Mint Julep is the traditional drink of the Ante-bellum South in the United States. There are several forms of this drink. Most are excellent and worthy of admiration but one, the Virginia Mint Julep, is outstanding and without peer. This superb drink, "the quintessence of gentlemanly beverages," combining a delightfully refreshing flavour with regional tradition and ceremony, holds a place of special honour in my home. We reserve it, along with our finest Highland Malt Whisky, for our most distinguished guests and closest friends. My great, great grand-uncle, General Richard Taylor, Confederate States Army, writing of his experiences in Virginia during the American Civil War, produced what has become the classic description of the mint julep "properly served." I always share this charming literary piece with my julep-drinking guests, who delight as much in Taylor's description as they do in partaking of the "nectar" of the Old South. I would like to introduce the recipe for the Virginia Mint Julep with General Taylor's description of it:

"A distant kinsman, whom I had never met, came to invite me to his house in the neighbourhood. Learning that I always slept in camp, he seemed so much distressed as to get my consent to breakfast with him, if he would engage to have breakfast at the barbarous hour of sunrise. His house was a little distant from the road; so, the following morning, he sent a mounted groom to show me the way . . .

"It was a fine old mansion, surrounded by well-kept grounds. This immediate region had not yet been touched by war. Flowering plants and rose trees, in full bloom, attested to the glorious wealth of June. On the broad portico, to welcome us, stood the host, with his fresh, charming wife, and, a little retired, a white-headed butler. Greetings over with host and lady, this delightful creature, with ebon face beaming hospitality, advanced holding a salver, on which rested a huge silver goblet filled with Virginia's nectar, mint julep.

"Quantities of cracked ice rattled refreshingly in the goblet; sprigs of fragrant mint peered above its broad rim; a mass of white sugar, too sweetly indolent to melt, rested on the mint; and, like rose buds on a snow bank, luscious strawberries crowned the sugar. Ah! that julep. Mars ne'er received such a tipple from the hands of Ganymede. Breakfast was announced, and what a breakfast! A beautiful service, snowy table cloth, damask napkins, long unknown; above all, a lovely woman in crisp gown, with more and handsomer roses on her cheek than in her garden. 'Twas an idyll in the midst of the stern realities of war!"

Into a well-chilled silver mint julep cup, place the leaves of two sprigs of mint. Cover these with two teaspoons of simple syrup. Thoroughly muddle the mint leaves and the simple syrup; then add one teaspoon of powdered sugar. Fill cup with finely-crushed ice and three ounces (or two jiggers) of any good straight or blended whisky (bourbon preferred). Gently jiggle the ice with a spoon, trying not to wet the outside of the cup, until the silver cup is well frosted, adding more ice as needed. Do not stir and do not hold cup with hand while jiggling ice. Decorate top of cup with two or three slightly

130

moist sprigs of fresh mint, which have been liberally sprinkled with white powdered sugar. These should project about 2 inches above the rim of the cup. Place small luscious strawberries on the sugar-coated mint leaves; slip a short straw into the ice; and serve on a silver salver.

Minty Carrots

12 medium size carrots
2 oz butter
1 tablespoon granulated sugar
1 teaspoon of white vinegar
1 tablespoon chopped mint (fresh or dried)
dash of salt

Scrape the carrots and cut into 2-inch lengths. Place these in a covered pan of boiling salt water and cook until tender. Drain and cut lengthwise. Melt the butter in a pan, add the sugar, vinegar, and mint; blend thoroughly. Put drained carrot slices in a well-greased baking dish; sprinkle lightly with salt; and cover with the mint mixture. Heat in a moderate oven (350° F, 180° C, Gas 4) for 15 minutes.

Bourbon Sweet Potatoes

½ stick (2 oz) butter
1 cup granulated sugar
⅓ cup bourbon whisky
1 teaspoon vanilla extract
3 lbs well-cooked sweet potatoes (if
  canned sweet potatoes are used, drain well)
miniature marshmallows

Melt butter; add sugar, bourbon and vanilla. Mash potatoes in a bowl. Add the bourbon-butter mixture and stir thoroughly. Spoon this mixture into a well greased casserole dish; and cover top with miniature marshmallows. Place in a moderate oven (350° F, 180° C, Gas 4) and heat until the marshmallows are melted.

Pear Water Ice (Sutherland).   132

Wallace

From Lt Col Malcolm R. Wallace of that Ilk, Hilton of Gask, Auchterarder, Perthshire

---

When I was first served with the hot butterscotch sauce with ice cream, my hostess's two small children were fascinated by the way the butterscotch sauce stuck to my moustache and the difficulty I had in disentangling myself from it. I only mention this as a warning!

Oxtail Soup

1 oxtail
2 quarts veal bone stock
salt and pepper
cloves

carrots
turnips
onions
2 tablespoons cornflour

Cut the oxtail into small pieces after washing with cold water. Put on heat with stock, boil quickly and stir. Add salt, pepper, and cloves in a muslin bag. Add cornflour, carrots, turnip and onions to soup half an hour before serving. Also add a little sherry before serving. Remove oxtail from soup.

Cooks: *This soup requires approximately 3 hours cooking. If possible, prepare the day before to the stage when thickening is added. This allows the fat to solidify on top and it is thus easily removed. On day of serving add the cornflour and vegetables and finish soup as recipe suggests.*

Hot Butterscotch Sauce

2 oz butter
4 oz caster sugar

¼ pint milk
1 tablespoon golden syrup

Boil and add few drops vanilla essence. Continue boiling and stirring until it is a pale golden brown.

The publishers gratefully acknowledge the financial assistance of Ronald Morrison & Co. Ltd. of Loanhead, near Edinburgh, in the publication of this volume. Ronald Morrison are the makers of the famous whisky-based liqueur

GLAYVA

Glayva is a whisky liqueur, the recipe for which is known by only three men—Michael and Gordon Morrison, whose family originated the recipe several generations ago and their Master Blender, Thomas Walker, who has blended every bottle of Glayva for the past 30 years.

Heather honey and specially grown herbs are added to the finest whiskies to produce this golden liqueur which is delicious either on its own, on ice or mixed in a cocktail. A few recipes are given for Glayva-based drinks which the men-folk in the family can mix while the women-folk tend the meal.

But Glayva also gives superb flavour to food, savoury as well as sweet. In the following collection of recipes, one of Scotland's top cookery experts, Mrs Ena Baxter from the famous Scottish food producing family—Baxter's of Speyside—has created eight dishes combining the unique flavour of Glayva with some of Baxter's most popular products. The result is mouth-watering dishes for special entertaining.

Ha' Hoose Sauce

2 tablespoons Baxters Cranberry Jelly
   or Sauce
2 tablespoons mango chutney
juice and grated rind of a lemon
1 tablespoon Glayva

Mix the Cranberry Jelly or Sauce with the mango chutney and the lemon juice and grated rind in a saucepan. Simmer together for 5 minutes until syrupy. Pour into a sauceboat or glass bowl and stir in the Glayva. Serve hot or cold.

Editor: *The name "Ha' Hoose" comes from the old North-East Scotland way of describing "The Hall" or "Manor House."*
   The sauce is piquant and fruity; it makes an excellent accompaniment for venison, roast or baked gammon.

135

Highland Mist

1 large egg yolk
1 oz (25 g) caster sugar
5 fl oz (150 ml) double cream
4-5 fl oz (150 ml) creamy milk
finely grated rind of ½ small lemon

1 heaped dessertspoon Baxters 3 Fruits
  Marmalade
2 dessertspoons Glayva
1 heaped dessertspoon toasted medium
  oatmeal

Beat the egg yolk and the sugar in a medium sized mixing bowl with an electric beater until very pale and creamy. Gradually add the cream and milk, beating continually until thick and velvety. Add the grated lemon rind and the marmalade and beat again until well mixed. Add the Glayva, keeping the mixture creamy and thick, then fold through the oatmeal. Chill until required. Serve in individual glass dishes.

   This is quite a rich dessert and small helpings are sufficient.

Turkey Cranberry Salad Ecosse

3 level teaspoons powdered gelatine
¼ pint (150 ml) water
2 tablespoons lemon juice
1 tablespoon Glayva
1 (8 oz) jar Baxters Cranberry Sauce
½ pint (300 ml) turkey stock
1 level tablespoon powdered gelatine
¼ teaspoon Tabasco sauce

2 tablespoons lemon juice
5 level tablespoons lemon mayonnaise
2 teaspoons finely chopped onion
2-3 sticks celery, chopped
1 small green pepper, chopped
1 red-skinned eating apple, diced
12 oz (300 g) cooked turkey, diced

Sprinkle 3 level teaspoons gelatine over the water in a bowl and stand this in a pan of hot water until dissolved. Add the lemon juice, Glayva and Cranberry Sauce, stir thoroughly until the sauce is completely melted; pour into a wetted mould and leave to set.

   Place the turkey stock in a pan, sprinkle 1 level tablespoon gelatine over the surface and dissolve over a low heat, but do not boil. Add the Tabasco sauce and lemon juice, pour into a bowl and leave to cool. Gradually whisk in the mayonnaise.

   When beginning to set, fold in the onion, celery, pepper, apple and turkey. Check the seasoning at this point.

   Spoon the mixture on to the cranberry layer and leave to set.

   Unmould to serve.

Vintage Liqueur Marmalade Flan

1 pastry flan case (see below)
2 oz (50 g) butter
12 oz (200 g) Baxters Vintage Marmalade
1 egg
1 tablespoon Glayva

Line a 9-inch flan case with shortcrust pastry rolled to about $\frac{1}{8}$-inch thick. Press to fit the bottom and sides; trim off surplus pastry with a sharp knife. Prick the pastry bottom well with a fork.

Melt the butter in a small saucepan; add the marmalade and beat till thoroughly blended. Add the well-beaten egg and the Glayva, stirring carefully. Do not let it boil. Pour this filling into the flan case.

Bake in a fairly hot oven 425°F, 220°C, Gas 7 for about 10 minutes, then reduce the heat to moderate (350°F, 180°C, Gas 4) and bake for 15 minutes longer until the mixture is set and the pastry is golden brown.

Serve cut in wedges accompanied by single cream to which you can add Glayva to taste.

Flan Case
4 oz (100 g) plain flour
pinch salt
3 oz (75 g) butter
1 level teaspoon (5 ml) caster sugar
1 egg yolk
cold water

Put flour and salt in mixing bowl and rub in the butter until mixture resembles fine breadcrumbs. Mix in sugar, add egg yolk and cold water if necessary to make a firm dough. Knead lightly.

Strawberry Compôte

Empty a tin of Baxters Strawberries into a glass bowl. Add 2 tablespoons orange juice and a liqueur glass of Glayva.

Stir well together and serve with small sponge fingers.

Speybank Favourite Fruit Mousse with Glayva

1 (15 oz) can Baxters Raspberries or
    Strawberries
juice of ½ lemon
½ oz (15 g) gelatine
3 eggs
2 oz (50 g) caster sugar
¼ pint (150 ml) double cream
1 tablespoon Glayva

To decorate
3-4 fl oz (100 ml) double cream
a little caster sugar to sweeten
2 teaspoons Glayva
a few crushed toasted almonds

Drain the syrup from the fruit and add the lemon juice; add the gelatine and dissolve over a gentle heat. Purée the fruit to remove the seeds.

Whisk the eggs and caster sugar together in a basin over hot water until thick and creamy and the whisk leaves a trail. Lightly whip the cream. To the egg mixture add the puréed fruit, the dissolved gelatine, the cream and the Glayva and fold all well together. Pour into a glass bowl to set.

Whip the remaining cream, sweeten to taste with sugar, add liqueur and pipe in a lattice over the top. Scatter the almonds over and serve.

Haddock with Lobster Sauce Glayva

1 can Baxters Lobster Bisque
2 lb (900 g) haddock fillet
juice of ½ lemon
2 oz (50 g) melted butter
pinch marjoram

½ level teaspoon salt
pinch white pepper
1 small carton cream
2 tablespoons Glayva

Wash the fish and cut into portions. Place in a shallow fireproof casserole, sprinkle with lemon juice and soak for 5-10 minutes. Drain off the juice. Pour the melted butter over the fish and sprinkle with the marjoram and seasonings. Grill for about 10 minutes, basting once.

Mix the Lobster Bisque with the cream and the Glayva, pour over the fish and cook for 30 minutes in the centre of a moderate oven (350°F, 180°C, Gas 4).

Liqueur Pancakes Framboise

Serves 4

4 oz (100 g) plain flour
pinch salt
1 large egg
¼ pint (150 ml) milk plus
   ¼ pint (150 ml) water, or use ½ pint (300 ml) milk
lard for frying
1 (15 oz) can Baxters Raspberries
1 rounded teaspoon cornflour
Glayva
1 small family block vanilla icecream

Sift flour and salt into a bowl. Make a well in the centre and add the egg. Mix in, then beat in half the milk and water until smooth. Now add the remainder.

Make four thin pancakes, using a non-stick pan, and rub a little lard on heated pan before frying the pancakes. Keep stacked flat with strips of greaseproof paper between.

Meanwhile empty the fruit into the pan and thicken with the cornflour, allow to boil for 3-4 minutes. Fill each warm pancake with a slice of ice cream, pour over a dessertspoon of Glayva. Fold up. Top with the glazed raspberries and serve at once.

Glayva-based Drinks

Mull of Kintyre

One part Glayva—serve in a tall glass with ice and lemon. Top with Coca-Cola and serve with straws.

Iced Gold

One measure of Glayva poured over ice.

Swinger

One part Glayva, five parts orange juice, a dash of lime. Serve on crushed ice.

Gold Mine

One part Glayva, one part Vodka, ice and a splash of soda. Decorate with slice of orange.

Chequered Flag

1 oz Glayva, ½ oz PLJ (lemon juice), 2 oz apple juice. Top up with American Ginger (or Tonic). Serve in 8 oz goblet with ice and lemon.

Index

A

Altyre Chicken, *34,* 40
Apple and Cranberry Steamed
    Pudding, 48
  —Cake, Easy, 85
Arbroath Smokie Cocottes, 75
Artichaut Froid "Carême",
    95, 97
Artichoke Soup, *22,* 86
Artillery Punch, 128
Atholl Brose, 108-9
Avocado Cheese, 60, *95*
  —Pudding, 57

B

Baked Chicken, 61
  —Limpets, 26
Baking
    Bessie MacAlpine's
        Chocolate Cake, 33
    Black Bun, 70
    Brownies, 81
    Carrot Bread, 63
    Chocolate Cake, 61
    Claire Mairi Hope's Marble
        Cake, 32
    Crunchies, 79
    Drop Scones (Pancake
        Scones), 69
    Easy Apple Cake, 85
    Economical Shortbread, 80
    Flapjacks, 106
    Ginger Cake, 45
    Granny Meikle's Christmas
        Cake, 93
    Kinloch Gâteau, *64, 66*
    Lady Mac's Special Cake, 80
    Rose Clan Shortbread, 118
    Shortbread, 87
    Spicy Crumb Cake, 79
    Sticky Gingerbread, 23
    Strawberry Shortcake, 33

    Tea Loaf, 81
    Victoria Sandwich, 87
Banniskirk Flummery, *51,* 55
Beef Stroganoff, 83
Beef, English Roast, 44
  —Roast, 124
  —Wellington, 94
  —with Cinnamon, 39, *82*
Bessie MacAlpine's Chocolate
    Cake, 33
Black Bun, 70
Bourbon Sweet Potatoes, 131
Brandied Raspberries, 18, *51*
Bread
    Carrot Bread, 63
    Potato Bread, 37
    Wheaten Loaf, *19,* 80
Bread and Butter Pudding, 9, 58
Breadcrumbs, Brown, 43
Brose, Atholl, 108-9
Brown Breadcrumbs, 43
Brownies, 81
Butterscotch Sauce, Hot, 133

C

Caledonian Cream, 18, *102*
Carrot Bread, 63
Carrots, Minty, 131
Casseroles
    Chestnut Stew, 70
    Chicken and Orange
        Casserole, 14
    Hare and Venison
        Casserole, 17
Champignons à la
    Normande, 68
Cheese dishes
    Avocado Cheese, 60, *95*
    Crowdie and Honey Tart,
        47, *51*

Kelburn Mousse, 21
Kirsch Cream Cheese, 59
Mum's Potted Sock, 25
Chestnut Soup, 125
  —Stew, 70
Chicken and Duck
    Altyre Chicken, *34,* 40
    Chicken and Orange
        Casserole, 13
    Chicken, Baked, 61
    Cold Chicken Lovat, 41
    Chicken Craighall, 113
    Chicken Paprika, 114
    Maigrets de Canard
        Sauvage, 97
    Nutty Chicken, 78
Chocolate Cake, 61
  —Cake, Bessie
        MacAlpine's, 33
  —Sauce, 44
Christmas Cake, Granny
    Meikle's, 93
Chutney, Plum, 100
Claire Mairi Hope's Marble
    Cake, 32
Clan Grant Special, 54
Coconut Cream, 115
Cold Chicken Lovat, 51
  —Orange Souffle, 16
  —Tomato Soup, 20, *22*
  —Snail Water, 58
  —Spinach Soufflé, 110
Crab Apple and Mint Jelly, 127
Crème Brûlée, 25
Cream, Caledonian, 18, *102*
  —Coconut, 115
  —Norwegian, 52
  —Pie, Whisky, *51,* 55
  —Smokies, 42
Crôute à la Findon, 31
Crowdie and Honey Tart, 47,
    51

Crunchies, 79
Cumberland Sauce, 29
Cure for Deafness, 116
Curried Apple Soup, 67
Curry, Mrs Nicholson's, 118

D

Devilled Grouse, 111
—Quails, 104
Deafness, Cure for, 116
Dresse Udders and Tongues,
    121
Drinks
    Artillery Punch, 128
    Atholl Brose, 108-9
    Ginger Beer, 117
    Virginia Mint Julep, 130
    Whisky Sour, 13
Drop Scones (Pancake Scones),
    69
Dundarve Steak and Kidney
    Pudding, *19, 91*
Dutch Pea Soup (Erwtensoep),
    22, 73

E

Easy Apple Cake, 85
Economical Shortbread, 80
Egg Mousse, 41, *95*
Eggs, Scotch, 84
English Roast Beef, 44

F

Fish Dishes
    Arbroath Smokie
        Cocottes, 75
    Cream Smokies, 42
    Croûte à la Findon, 31
    Fish Pie, 105
    —Soup, 123
    Haddock with Lobster
        Sauce Glayva, 138
    Kipper Pâté, 28, 61
    Mackerel Pâté, *19,* 126
    River Add Salmon, *88-9,* 98
    Salmon Plait, *19,* 110
    Sister Lucy's Salmon
        Mousse, 34,

Sister Catherine's Salmon
    Mousse, 34, *95*
Flapjacks, 106
Flat Rock Pudding, *51,* 129
Flummery, Banniskirk, *51, 55*
    —Highland, 20
Fool, Raspberry, *51,* 87

G

Game Dishes
    Devilled Grouse, 111
    —Quails, 104
    Hare and Venison
        Casserole, 17
    Italian Pheasant with
        Cream, 49
    Jubilee Venison, 29
    Raised Game Pie, *19,* 30
    Roast Grouse, 43
    Spare Orrels, 27
Gaspacho, *22,* 116
Gâteau, Kinloch, *64, 66*
Ginger Beer, 117
    —Cake, 45
Gingerbread, Sticky, 23
Glayva, 135-141
Granny Meikle's Christmas
    Cake, 93
Granny's Scotch Broth, 9, 107
Green Butter, 31
Grouse, Devilled, 111
    —Roast, 43

H

Ha' Hoose Sauce, 135
Haddock with Lobster Sauce
    Glayva, 138
Ham Steaks, 76
Hare and Venison Casserole, 17
Helva, 83
Highland Flummery, 20
    —Mist, 136
Hot Butterscotch Sauce, 133

I

Italian Pheasant with
    Cream, 49

J

Jelly, Crab Apple and
    Mint, 127
Jubilee Venison, 29
Julep, Virginia Mint, 130

K

Kelburn Mousse, 21
Kinloch Gâteau, *64, 66*
Kipper Pâté, 28, 61
Kirsch Cream Cheese, 59

L

Lady Mac's Special Cake, 80
Lamb, Roast Leg of, 127
Leeks au Gratin, 86
Lemon Fluff, Mrs Patrick's, 90
    —Pudding, 92
Lettuce Floats, 91, *95*
Limpets, Baked, 26
Liqueur Pancakes
    Framboise, 139
Loaf, Wheaten, *19,* 80

M

Macaroni Salad, Sister
    Catherine's, 34
Mackerel Pâté, *19,* 126
Maigrets de Canard
    Sauvage, 97
Maple Parfait, 24
Marble Cake, Claire Mairi
    Hope's, 32
Marinade for Barbecue Lamb
    Chops, 106
    —for Venison, 21
Marinated Venison Steaks, 112
Marmalade, 100
    —Flan, Vintage Liqueur,
    102, 137
Meat Dishes
    Beef Stroganoff, 83
        —Wellington, 96
        —with Cinnamon, 39, 82
    Dundarve Steak and Kidney
        Pudding, *19,* 91

Dresse Udders and
 Tongues, 121
English Roast Beef, 44
Ham Steaks, 76
Mrs Davidson's Loin of Pork
 with Piquant Sauce, 121
Mrs Nicholson's Curry, 118
Oxtail, 53
Peppers Stuffed with Veal, 85
Roast Beef, 124
 —Leg of Lamb, 127
Spare Ribs in Bar-B-Que
 Sauce, 62
Steak au Poivre, 116
Turkey Cranberry Salad
 Ecosse, *102*, 136
Melon Starter, 57, *95*
Minty Carrots, 131
Miss MacEchern's Seaweed
 Pudding, 120
Mousses
 Egg—41, *95*
 Kelburn—, 21
 Sister Lucy's Salmon—, 32
 Speybank Favourite Fruit—
  with Glayva, *102*, 138
 Susan Catherine's
  Salmon—, 34, 95
Mrs Davidson's Loin of Pork
 with Piquant Sauce, 121
 —Nicholson's Curry, 118
 —Patrick's Lemon Fluff, 90
Mum's Potted Sock, 25

N

Norwegian Cream, 52
Nun's Pudding, 52
Nutty Chicken, 78

O

Omelette Rothschild, 97
Orange
 Chicken and—Casserole, 13
 Cold—Souffle, 16
Oxtail, 53
 —Soup, *22*, 133

P

Pancakes, Liqueur Framboise,
 139
Parfait, Maple, 24
 Parkins, 42
Pâté
 Kipper—, 28, 61
 Mackerel—, *19*, 126
 Smoked Trout or Smoked
  Mackerel—, 126
Pavlova, Worcesterberry, 74
Pea Soup, 94
 —Dutch (Erwtensoep), *22*,
  73
Pear Water Ice, 127, *132*
Peppers Stuffed with Veal, 85
Pheasant with Cream,
 Italian, 49
Pies
 Fish—, 105
 Raised Game—, *19*, 30
 Rowan—, 31
 Tarte a l'Oignon, *19*, 77
 Whisky Cream—, *51*, 105
Plum Chutney, 101
Pork, Loin of, Mrs Davidson's,
 121
Porridge, 122
Potato Bread, 37
 —Soup, 99
Potted Shrimps, 17
Prawns, Whisky, 103
Puddings
 Apple and Cranberry
  Steamed Pudding, 48
 Avocado Pudding, 57
 Banniskirk Flummery, *51*, 55
 Brandied Raspberries, 18, *51*
 Caledonian Cream, 18, *102*
 Coconut Cream, 115
 Crème Brûlée, 25
 Crowdie and Honey Tart,
  47, *51*
 Flat Rock Pudding, *51*, 129
 Highland Flummery, 20
  —Mist, 136
 Kirsch Cream Cheese, 59
 Lemon Pudding, 92
 Liqueur Pancakes
  Framboise, 139

Maple Parfait, 24
Miss MacEchern's Seaweed
 Pudding, 120
Mrs Patrick's Lemon Fluff,
 90
Norwegian Cream, 52
Nun's Pudding, 52
Pear Water Ice, 20, *132*
Raspberry Fool, *51*, 87
Rødgrød, 77
Speybank Favourite Fruit
 Mousse with Glayva,
 102, 138
Strawberry Compôte, 137
Worcesterberry Pavlova, 75
Punch, Artillery, 128

Q

Quails, Devilled, 104

R

Raised Game Pie, *19*, 30
Raspberries, Brandied, 18, *51*
Raspberry Fool, *51*, 87
Ravioli Verdi, 38
Rhubarb Pudding, 113
Rissoles, Salmon, 56
River Add Salmon, 88-9, 98
Roast Beef, 124
 —Beef, English, 44
 —Grouse, 43
 —Leg of Lamb, 127
 —Venison, 46
Rødgrød, 77
Rose Clan Shortbread, 118
Rowan Pie, 31

S

Salmon
 —Mousse, Sister Lucy's, 32
 —Mousse, Susan
  Catherine's, 34, *95*
 —Plait, *19*, 110
 —Rissoles, 56
 —River Add, 88-9, 98

Sauces
    Cumberland—, 29
    Chocolate—, 44
    Ha' Hoose—, 135
    Hot Butterscotch—, 133
    Salsa Verde, 39
Scampi, Super, 60
Scones, Drop (Pancakes), 69
Scotch Broth, Granny's, 107
    —Eggs, 84
Seafood Dishes
    Baked Limpets, 26
    Potted Shrimps, 17
    Super Scampi, 60
    Whisky Prawns, 103
Seal Hoosh, 14
Seaweed Pudding, Miss
    MacEchern's, 120
Sheriff Soup, 15, *22*
Shortbread, 87
    —Economical, 80
    —Rose Clan, 118
Shortcake, Strawberry, 33
Shrimps, Potted, 17
Sister Catherine's Macaroni
    Salad, 34
    —Lucy's Salmon Mousse, 32
Skirley, 18
Smoked Trout or Smoked
    Mackerel Pâté, 126
Smokies, Cream, 42
Soups
    Artichoke—, *22*, 86
    Chestnut—, 125
    Chief's Tomato—, 54
    Clan Grant Special, 54
    Cold Tomato—, 20, *22*
    Curried Apple—, 67
    Dutch Pea—(Erwtensoep),
    22, 73
    Fish—, 123
    Gaspacho, *22*, 116

Granny's Scotch Broth, 9,
    107
Oxtail—, *22*, 133
Pea—, 94
Potato—, 99
Sheriff—, 15, *22*
Tarator, 84
Tomato—, *19*, 72
Sour Crout, 117
Spare Orrels, 27
Spare Ribs in Bar-B-Que
    Sauce, 62
Speybank Favourite Fruit
    Mousse with Glayva, *102*
    138
Spicy Crumb Cake, 79
Spinach Soufflé, Cold, 110
Starters
    Arbroath Smokie Cocottes,
    75
    Artichaut Froid
    "Carême", *95*, 97
    Avocado Cheese, 60, *95*
    Cream Smokies, 42
    Croute à la Findon, 31
    Kipper Pâté, 28, 61
    Lettuce Floats, 91, *95*
    Mackerel Pâté, *19*, 126
    Melon Starter, 57, *95*
    Potted Shrimps, 17
    Smoked Trout or Smoked
    Mackerel Pâté, 126
Steak and Kidney Pudding,
    Dundarve, 91
    —au Poivre, 116
Steaks, Ham, 76
Stew, Chestnut, 70
Sticky Gingerbread, 23
Strawberry Compôte, 137
    —Shortcake, 33
Stuffed Shoulder of Venison,
    47

Super Scampi, 60
Susan Catherine's Salmon
    Mouse, 34, *95*
Sweet Potatoes, Bourbon, 131

T

Tarator, 84
Tart, Crowdie and Honey,
    47, *51*
Tarte à l'Oignon, *19*, 77
Tea Loaf, 81
Tomato Soup, *19*, 72
    — —Cold, 20, *22*
    — —Chief's, 54
Tortilla con Patatas, 123
Turkey Cranberry Salad
    Ecosse, *102*, 136

V

Veal, Peppers Stuffed with, 85
Venison
    Jubilee—, 29
    Marinade for—, 21
    Marinated—Steaks, 112
    Roast—, 46
    Spare Orrels, 27
    Stuffed Shoulder of—, 47
    Venison, 75
    —Pie, 100
Victoria Sandwich, 87
Vintage Liqueur Marmalade
    Flan, *102*, 137
Virginia Mint Julep, 130

W

Wheaten Loaf, *19*, 80
Whisky Cream Pie, *51*, 55
    —Prawns, 103
    —Sour, 13
Worcesterberry Pavlova, 74

Dishes illustrated in colour are indicated by italic numerals